# Update

### Federal Republic of

# Germany

Other titles in this series:

# Update

## Federal Republic of

# Germany

Nessa P. Loewenthal

Alison R. Lanier was the originator of the Update series and is currently editor of *The International American,* a monthly newsletter for Americans living and working abroad.

Intercultural Press, Inc.
Yarmouth, Maine

For information, contact
Intercultural Press, Inc.
P.O. Box 700
Yarmouth, ME 04096 USA

Library of Congress Catalog No. 89-082120
ISBN 0-933662-86-6

Printed in the United States of America

# Table of Contents

# Foreword

Some months ago, after this Update, originally entitled *Update Federal Republic of Germany*, had been completed, the "impossible dream" of German unity began to unfold as The Wall was first breached and then torn down. November 9, 1989 has become a date which will be remembered and celebrated in history.

The beginning of the end was the summer of 1989. Youthful East Germans, primarily intellectuals and professionals, disenchanted with the existing political, social, and economic realities of their lives, left the country on holiday, sought refuge in the Embassy of the Federal Republic of Germany or FRG (West Germany) in Hungary, and finally made their way to the FRG, entering as refugees. In September, members of the "silent majority," who had previously talked only among themselves, decided to speak out. This group of intellectuals formed an organization called the New Forum; they organized demonstrations and provided leadership to those in opposition to the communist regime. Jens Reich, one of the founders of the New Forum and a committed socialist, explained the new willingness to risk exposure and even life itself: "You don't need courage to speak out against a regime. You just need not to care anymore—not to care about being punished or beaten.... We reached the point where enough people just didn't care anymore what would happen if they spoke out."

In the early days of freedom, the question of unification with the "other Germany" was accompanied by fear: fear that the 16.y million people of the German Democratic Republic or GDR (East Germany), along with the country itself, would be swallowed up by West Germany; fear that the material and moral values of its egalitarian, collectivist society would be lost. There was also hope: hope for the future, hope for freedom of decision and of movement. Many East Germans crossed the border to reaffirm their hopes for change at home rather than in flight. One woman said she would go to West Berlin as a tourist, but "our life is here. Besides, someone has to stay behind and change things. Everyone can't leave."

The forced division of East and West Germany is a thing of the past, but the problems inherent in creating a new union are becoming apparent and are a cause of concern—particularly to the East Germans, who must bear most of the burden of change. In the process, citizens from both East and West are becoming aware of the differences between them, which may take years to over-come—if they are overcome at all.

The euphoria initially experienced by both sides has disap-peared as the realities of everyday life become evident, generally expressed in terms of loss and/or fear. In an effort to quiet peoples' fears, the East German leadership issued an appeal to the population to develop a society of solidarity in which peace and social justice, individual freedom, freedom of movement, and the preservation of the environment are guaranteed. Egon Krenz, former Prime Minister, committed the government to rehabilitating socialism with a heavy dose of democracy and environmentalism.

In the Federal Republic, dreams of unification compete with the fear of political and life style changes. These fears and concerns continue despite reassurances offered by Chancellor Kohl and the Christian Democratic Union (CDU). As of September 18, 1989—before the fall of the wall—the unemployment rate was 7.5 percent, and housing shortages already existed in all major cities. The influx of the East Europeans, including East Germans, is causing concern about the future direction and leadership of the Federal Republic; polls reveal that the East Germans and other immigrants/refugees tend to favor the more conservative ideas of the Nationalist and Christian Democrats over those of the Social Democratic party. This information is, in fact, the basic reason for the speed with which the economic and political unification is taking place. Chancellor Kohl badly wants to be known as the first chancellor of a united Germany. In an effort to benefit from the conservative leanings of the East Germans, he pushed up the date for economic unification to July 7, 1990 and set 1990 as the date for political unification. A Frankfurt paper summarizes the views of many in the East and West: "...The train of German unification is moving so fast that at times it seems to have arrived before departure times have even been announced...." It is feared that the CDU, Kohl's party, may lose its advantage as the predicted economic problems in the East become more apparent.

Unification is threatening to other Western nations as well. The leaders of these nations have long felt that the stability of Europe rested on two German states—one tied to the East and one to the West. There is also fear that unification will be the beginning of the Fourth Reich, the rebirth of "The Fatherland." This is a fear that both the GDR and FRG want to lay to rest. There is no thought, in the minds of the leaders, of reviving the German nationalism that existed from 1871 to 1945. When Germans look back at that period, they see war, death, delusion, and tragedy. This retrospective perception explains why most Germans are not thinking about redrawing maps.

There is also a positive, practical perspective—the Federal Republic needs immigrants. Its population is stagnant and aging rapidly. Demographic forecasts show that it will lose 10 percent of its population in the next thirty years. This trend has already been felt—in 1989, 200,000 apprenticeships went unfilled. Those companies which have taken advantage of the recent influx of Eastern European refugees feel that they add dynamism to the economy and to society at large, that they are highly reliable and quickly become productive members of the workforce. In fact, FRG government economists are predicting that the current burden of resettlement will be quickly repaid by the income produced from social security and income tax payments from this new addition to the workforce.

In order to be successful and long lasting, unification must occur on many levels, including economic, political, social, and cultural.

Economic unification was accomplished on July 7, 1990, when the Deutsche mark became the official currency of the GDR. When the supporters of the New Forum dreamed of (and marched for) freedom and unity with West Germany they were driven more by economics than by politics. They were seeking better jobs, more discretionary income, and higher living standards—what some called "Mercedes democracy." East Germany will quickly become an important part of the Federal Republic's economy because it is a source of low-cost labor and provides a ready market for products. Along with economic unification are problems which must be recognized and dealt with: unemployment due to the closing of plants and cutbacks in military forces; the need for East Germans to pay for services and necessities which had been provided at a controlled cost—mortgages, rent, heat, bread; concern about job security; and the realities of inflation and higher taxes.

In spite of the problems, there is hope in the GDR. By the end of May 1990, 59,435 new companies and businesses had been registered; several American subsidiaries were establishing themselves, utilizing facilities formerly occupied by government-owned cartels; and West German firms ranging from banks to construction companies were rushing to establish businesses or joint ventures. The West German government has committed large sums of money to assist in undoing the damage to city infrastructures, housing, and the environment resulting from forty years of neglect. Above all, the economic union will work because both sides are committed to its success.

Political unification is scheduled, at least on the surface, for October 3, when general elections are being held in East and West. One concern, expressed by both the East and West is that those who initiated the downfall of the previous regime in the GDR, those who make up the New Forum, are intellectuals, not politicians, and therefore will probably not be elected to the joint parliament. This is coupled with a fear that, because of the lack of trained political leadership, democracy could deteriorate into a politics of personality, which would not be in the best interests of the German nation, the European Community, or the world.

The fact that three-quarters of the East Germans believe that the state is, and should continue to be, responsible for their welfare is an indication of the problems involved in social unification. In order to meet the needs of those who hold this perception, the social policies of the new Germany must be changed. There are also strongly differing perceptions of individual responsibility for the environment, for the overall quality of life, and for the role of the individual as a member of society.

George Kennan describes "romantic linguistic nationalism" as a belief that a common language creates a community. Many observers feel that the Germans have subscribed to this point of view for more than a century and that, in fact, cultural unification will remain a myth, that the creation of one culture from many—if possible—will take at least three generations to achieve. The shared values of the two Germanys are those espoused by Luther and Goethe. Many of the differences between the two societies are political and economic and will change over time, but the deeper the value, the greater the difference.

it is interesting to note that the East German fits the stereotype of "The German" much more closely than does the West German. It is the East German who is spartan, puritanical, innocent, and who lives in a homogeneous society. In West Germany, during the forty years of separate existence, many traditional "German" biases have disappeared. The West German of today is more European than German, according to Elizabeth Boelle-Neuman of the Allensbach Research Institute. "We care about the Third World and the environment. We have a peace movement. We value opposing views."

Irene Runge, an East German sociologist, says: "Decades of socialism have reinforced our worst traits. We East Germans are more respectful of authority, less flexible, and less accepting of individual differences than we were before the war." In East Germany, as in most of the Eastern Bloc countries where nationalism has been repressed, nationalistic groups are beginning to reappear. Runge continues, "Xenophobia runs deep among East Germans. We will not make very good democrats." Visitors to the cities report being surrounded by skinheads shouting, *"Auslander raus!"*

No one can predict what will happen, or when, but whatever happens in the process of unification, there is agreement on the part of the Federal Republic and other Western nations—including the United States—that the German situation needs a European solution; that, as a collective European issue, change can be managed peacefully and in the best interest of all. The Foreign Ministry of the Federal Republic explained that its goal is "to bring about West European integration...with the idea that the German question will solve itself within a confederated Europe." It is also apparent that the stability of each nation and of Europe is a primary concern.

The dream of a unified Germany has been kept alive through the years by the hope of a new and united nation—living in peace with each other and with its neighbors. This new Germany is described by Helmut Kohl as "embedded in the European security architecture," and as a "transit point for ideas and perspectives between the East and the West." The realization of this dream depends on the ability of Germany's leaders to bring the economy of East Germany in line with that of the FRG.

The opportunities and challenges available to U.S. and FRG businesses are being recognized and acted upon, but it is essential that those involved also recognize that changes must meet the needs of the East Germans, that change doesn't occur overnight, and, if forced, it will be costly and ineffective over the long run.

It is also critical that the differences in deep-seated attitudes and values, in perceptions and behaviors be recognized, accepted, and respected. In order to function effectively and to succeed in today's global economy, those involved in interactions with people from other cultures need to be aware of the existence of these differences and prepared to accept the challenge of working with them.

Helmut Kohl, speaking for himself and his government, said: "...When the historic moment allows it, let us have the unity of our country. The right of self-determination that belongs to all countries belongs also to Germans."

Nessa P. Loewenthal
September 1, 1990

# 1

# Background

## OVERVIEW

The Federal Republic of Germany (FRG) is hardly what one would call a large country. From the northern border to its southern tip is only a seventy-minute flight and from east to west, thirty minutes; in area it is about the size of Ecuador or Yugoslavia, a little less than 96,000 square miles. Although some ten million people live in Ecuador and about twenty-four million live in Yugoslavia, the population of the FRG is over sixty million, according to the 1989 estimate. Almost a quarter of the population lives in villages of fewer than two thousand people while more than five million are concentrated in the three largest cities: Hamburg (1.6 million), West Berlin (1.8 million), and München (Munich) (1.3 million). Six smaller cities have populations topping a half-million each: Köln (Cologne), Essen, Düsseldorf, Frankfurt, Dortmund, and Stuttgart.

### Geographic Regions

The Federal Republic falls rather neatly into six main geographic regions: the north, the west or Rhineland, the Ruhr, Frankfurt am Main, Bavaria, and West Berlin.

**The North** comprises a highly industrialized port area which includes the active seaports of Hamburg (Germany's largest city and most important port) and Bremerhaven, plus the major cities

1

of Bremen (home of Beck's beer), Kiel, Lübeck, and Hanover.

**The West or Rhineland**, an area familiar to tourists, is bordered by Holland, Belgium, Luxembourg, and France. Here lies the wide Rhine valley with its picturesque castles and vineyards—a main thoroughfare for freight-carrying river barges.

**The Ruhr** is the home of Europe's heavy industry, where Essen, Dortmund, Mülheim, and other cities merge under smoke-laden skies, forming a densely populated megalopolis. On the nearby Rhine are Duisburg (Europe's largest inland port), Düsseldorf, and Köln.

**Frankfurt am Main** and its southern neighbors, Stuttgart and Mannheim, form another prosperous industrial area. Frankfurt is the country's financial center and the site of many trade fairs.

**Bavaria** is known worldwide for tourism, vineyards, wine, and rugged mountain scenery; the music, spas, skiing, and picturesque cities of the region, like München and Nürnberg (Nuremberg), delight its visitors. Although light and precision industries are concentrated in Bavaria, there is none of the heavy industry that is found in the north.

**West Berlin**, the second largest city in the Federal Republic, is an industrial and commercial center and is a ready market for consumer goods.

Even though the FRG is a leading industrial nation, 54 percent of its land remains either as pasture or cropland and another 29 percent is forest—all in all, a pleasant and varied landscape. The industrialized areas are highly concentrated. Beyond them are medieval cities, vineyards, broad river valleys, and old-world towns dominated by fortified castles, where one can forget the traffic, sprawl, and confusion of the major cities.

## Rivers

Germany's rivers and canals form a superb water transport system, which is vital to commerce and connects the Federal Republic with the rest of Europe.

The Rhine, source of many a poem and song, is the greatest waterway, originating in Switzerland and emptying into the North

Sea 537 miles away in The Netherlands. With its two main tributaries (the Moselle and the Main), the Rhine links southwest Germany to the Dutch Lowlands and the sea.

Three eastern rivers also flow into the North Sea and each has its port city: the Ems (Emden), the Weser (Bremen/Bremerhaven), and the Elbe (Hamburg).

In southern Germany the Danube flows 402 miles from west to east into Austria and Hungary, linking Germany to Central Europe and the Black Sea.

Connecting these large, natural waterways is a network of canals, of which the most recently constructed is the Rhine-Main-Danube canal, a shipping route that links the mouth of the Rhine in Holland with the mouth of the Danube in the Black Sea.

## Climate

The Federal Republic of Germany's climate, although considered moderate, tends to be more rigorous than that of Britain. Most of southern Germany shares the same latitude as the city of Quebec, Canada, and even further north. This makes for dark, long winter days but lovely, long summer evenings.

Wherever you are in the FRG, the weather changes frequently, even in the course of a day. Rainfall is consistent throughout the year, with cold winds in the winter. It seldom gets excessively hot; even in the summer, a warm sweater may be needed. Temperatures vary according to altitude and proximity to the sea. Snow falls frequently between December and March, and many of the higher areas from the Harz Mountains to the Alps are snow-covered all year. The wind-chill factor makes it seem even colder than the thermometer indicates because of the wind and the ever present dampness.

## THE PEOPLE

Conservative, hard-working, formal and reserved, disciplined, clean, efficient, duty-bound—these are among the characteristics for which Germans are known. If this sounds drab, remember that Germans are also known for their ability to enjoy life fully, particularly with their families, around which most of their social life revolves.

The Germans share a common heritage, combining Teutonic strains (similar to those of the Scandinavians) with Latin and Slavic elements. And since Germany shares borders with ten different nations, there is an intermingling of cultures, especially along the frontiers.

German society is dominated by its middle class, which prides itself on its ability to manage a densely populated land and a burgeoning economy effectively, a model of Western capitalism.

The population recently reached 61 million people, with 646 people per square mile, even though the birthrate is low (0.2 percent) and still declining. This crowding is partially the result of two major migrations since 1949, which added an estimated fifteen million people to the population: an influx of about thirteen million people from the eastern part of Germany and nearly four million *Gastarbeiters* (guest workers) from the south. (Added to this are the thousands of NATO troops—mostly from the United States—based in Germany.) By 1986 the number of foreign workers in Germany had reached almost four million, even though since 1973 and the oil crisis, the inward flow of workers has been restricted almost entirely to nationals from other EEC countries: Turks, Yugoslavs, Italians, Danes, and Greeks. Several demographers have predicted that because of the low birthrate, the population of the FRG by the year 2010 will be around thirty-five million, of which fewer than half will be of working age.

Whatever their nationality, all employees and their dependents automatically become members of the Federal Republic's social security system. To insure that all foreigners employed by a German enterprise receive the many benefits to which they are entitled, the local social security office must be informed immediately of their employment. Social security agreements have been signed with other nations, including the U.S., all EEC countries (Belgium, Denmark, Greece, France, Ireland, Italy, Luxembourg, The Netherlands, and the United Kingdom), as well as most other Western European countries, Canada, Poland, and Romania.

## FAMOUS GERMANS

Every country has a roster of people to whom its inhabitants point with pride. Making such a selection for Germany is difficult because Germany has produced so many outstanding individuals that it is hard to select who should be included in such a list. Several have been significant not only in German history but in the development of Western culture as well.

Credit for publishing and mass literacy goes to **Johann Gutenberg**, who invented the first European printing press with movable type.

Others who changed history include **Martin Luther**, leader of the Protestant Reformation; two great philosophers, **Immanuel Kant** and **Georg Hegel**; and **Albert Einstein**, who formulated the theory of relativity.

There is a stream of great composers, including **Johann Sebastian Bach**, **Johannes Brahms**, **Ludwig van Beethoven**, and **Richard Wagner**.

Among the greatest of Germany's many renowned authors are **Johann von Goethe**, **Heinrich Heine**, and **Heinrich Böll**.

**Albrecht Dürer** and **Hans Holbein** rank with the great masters in art. **Franz Marc** and **Max Ernst** are significant in the development of modern art, and **Walter Gropius** is a well-known architect.

Two of Germany's greatest military and political leaders were **Bismarck** and **Frederick II**.

**Wilhelm Roentgen** discovered the X-ray; **Robert Koch** developed the tuberculin test; **Hermann von Helmholtz** applied the law to conserve energy to mathematics; and **Max Planck** worked out the quantum theory in thermodynamics.

Even if you don't know about any of these people in great detail, you should be aware of their names and able to identify their major achievements. This will endear you to your German hosts, who will recognize and appreciate the fact that you are interested in them and have made an effort to learn about that which is important to them.

## THE GOVERNMENT

The Federal Republic of Germany was established in 1949, when a constitution was drawn up by a consultative assembly of state representatives. Its Parliament operates somewhat differently from the U.S. Congress, even though it has two houses, the Federal Council (*Bundesrat*) and the Federal Diet (*Bundestag*).

The Bundesrat, which is the upper house of the Parliament, consists of forty-one voting delegates, each of whom has one vote, and four nonvoting observers from West Berlin. Every state has at least three votes and the larger ones have up to five. Presidents of various *Länder* (who are automatically members of the Bundesrat) take turns serving as its president. Thus, all the Länder have direct representation at the federal level through this system of Länder government appointment and recall of delegates to the Bundesrat. The Bundesrat approves or disapproves legislation passed by the Bundestag.

The Bundestag, the lower house, is the principal legislative body, passing the laws and selecting the head of government. Its 496 voting representatives and twenty-two nonvoting observers from West Berlin are elected to four-year terms by the people of their Länder.

The chancellor, who is also a member of the Bundestag, is elected by a majority of its members. He not only determines the general policy of the country but can also both propose and remove the federal ministers (who conduct the business of federal departments) with a great deal more autonomy than is known in the U.S. Because of these roles, the chancellor is extremely powerful. Although the Bundestag does not have the power to remove federal ministers, it does have the power to remove the chancellor through a vote of no confidence; this acts as a control and balance of power within the government.

Technically, the head of state is the federal president, but he plays a very limited, mostly ceremonial role. For example, although he signs treaties and laws, they must be countersigned by the chancellor and by the federal minister concerned. The president is elected for a term of five years by a special Federal Assembly convened for that purpose, and he can be reelected.

The federal government is responsible for such matters as national defense, federal finance, transportation, and communications. Diplomats are assigned by the Foreign Ministry, foreign policy is formulated by the chancellor and foreign minister, and treaties are negotiated by the Foreign Ministry or the ministry that has jurisdiction in the specific matters involved.

The Länder have control over education, cultural affairs, justice, and public safety. Within each Länd, local communes (neighborhood councils) have considerable autonomy and the responsibility for administering their own affairs. Cities have a city council, mayor (*Bürgermeister*), and cabinet, all elected. Every municipality (*Gemeinde*) elects a mayor as well. Each county (*Ländkreis*) elects a commissioner (*Ländrat*) who is responsible to the state government.

## THE CURRENT POLITICAL SCENE

Since World War II, two key coalitions have dominated the political scene. Two political coalitions have each ruled Germany during the postwar years, one made up of the Social Democratic party (SPD) and the Free Democratic party (FDP), the other composed of the Christian Democratic Union (CDU) and the Christian Social Union (CSU). The latter (CDU/CSU) is now in power. At one time there was an effective coalition between the SPD and the CDU.

The general election in January 1987 confirmed the mandate of the coalition of conservatives (CDU) and liberals (CSU) to continue leading Germany. The federal chancellor, Helmut Kohl, retained a stable majority in the new Bundestag despite a considerable loss of votes for his party. Kohl's relative youth and length of service in the government convinced the public that he was sufficiently levelheaded to provide competent and stable leadership.

In March 1987 the federal chancellor outlined for the Bundestag the principles and objectives of his government's policy for the next four years in three areas of concentration: home policy, Germany, and foreign policy.

## Home Policy

The focus of the home policy is described as follows:

**Freedom and responsibility** together form the foundation of society, and awareness of these values must be sharpened. Without a legal order that is respected by all, there will be no free individual development or internal peace.

**Protection of the environment** is a major priority for the nation and is to be written into the constitution. A broad range of legislative and other measures is planned to ensure the preservation of the natural foundation of life—clean air and clean water. People have a right to live in a clean environment, but everyone must contribute through his or her own behavior. Protection of the environment starts at home.

**The social market economy** is the best possible economic order to assure equality of opportunity, prosperity, environmental protection, and social progress. Self-initiative and a spirit of enterprise are its foundation. They are indispensable prerequisites for successfully fighting the continuing problem of unemployment. Comprehensive tax reform is planned to ease the burden of the taxpayers and contribute to individual initiative.

## Germany

FRG policy focuses on the unity of the German nation and the preservation of the common national heritage. The government of the Federal Republic is committed to doing all it can to expand relations between the two German states, to create and maintain an open climate for communication, and to improve the contacts between the peoples of the Federal Republic and the German Democratic Republic.

Germans want to proclaim "we are our own people" but must at the same time embrace the defense of Europe and deal with the realization that all of Western Europe is affected by their economic decisions.

It is at the border between the two German states that the complexity and seriousness of Europe's division comes into sharpest focus. This is **the** border between East and West, and all Germans have always been aware of the possibility that a war could begin here—or that they could be the first to experience new initiatives in constructive relationships between East and West. Naturally, West Germans have had a special interest in ending the arms race and in any events that indicate a change in the political climate.

## Foreign Policy

The foreign policy of the Federal Republic of Germany is one of fostering global peace, and its security rests on the Atlantic Alliance. The political, economic, and cultural future of the Federal Republic depends on a united Europe; therefore, the primary objective of its European policy is the further development of the European Community into a European Union. Its policy towards the Soviet Union is to work towards more understanding and cooperation—particularly in the field of disarmament and arms control—while guaranteeing the security of all.

Germany is an advocate for the development of the Third-World countries, viewing them as partners with equal rights whose drive for independence and self-determination must be supported. Aid to developing nations is considered a task of society as a whole that must involve private as well as governmental initiative and involvement.

## ECONOMY

In the aftermath of World War II, Germany lay in ruins. It had been defeated politically and militarily, much of its industry had been destroyed, and its economy was in a state of chaos. It is now the dominant economic power in Europe—so much so that many Europeans are both wary and envious. Having weathered the economic ups and downs of the 1970s and 1980s, Germany is today the world's leading exporter of manufactured goods and has one of the world's most stable currencies.

The FRG trades extensively within the Common Market, of which it is one of the original members, and with the rest of Europe and the United States. It accounts for almost 10 percent of total world trade and is the second largest trading nation after the U.S. The United States ranks fifth as Germany's supplier and customer while Germany is America's third largest supplier and customer.

The German middle class is stable and has greatly expanded in recent years due to the general prosperity, generous employment benefits, and tax credits for home ownership (40 percent of the Germans are home owners).

Most people are employed in business and industry or in public service. Only about 15 percent work in agriculture and related industries or are self-employed. Thus, when the business economy suffers, there are severe repercussions. The standard of living has risen dramatically since 1950, but all Germans now feel the pressure of increasing inflation. The rapid economic growth of the seventies has recently fallen victim to an economic slowdown and to vigorous competition from Japan in the sale of manufactured goods. The gross national product, on the rise for all of the seventies, is falling, and West German spirits are sagging with the statistics.

Labor-related issues are among Germany's thorniest problems. And one of those issues is the very generous benefit package that German workers have obtained through social legislation. Illness is compensated by full wages for six weeks and 75-80 percent thereafter from health insurance funds. Nearly everyone is covered for major medical and dental costs. Pension plans are written to include adjustments for both inflation and the rising average wages of fellow workers and self-employed people, including housewives. For the first year, unemployment benefits equal 68 percent of a worker's salary, and welfare benefits total 58 percent of former pay. Vacation benefits are also very liberal. But those benefits take a large bite out of the workers' paychecks and impose a heavy burden upon both business and government. The social programs, once affordable, are now the albatross around the German neck.

A second labor issue is unemployment, which, at over 10 percent, is the worst since the postwar years. Labor problems are a national disease and are slowly sapping strength from the German economy. In the late 1960s a shortage of labor led to the recruitment of large numbers of foreign workers who, together with their families, now account for almost 7 percent of the German population. In 1973 recruitment of foreign labor except from Common Market countries was banned in an effort to relieve the strain on the economy. All foreign workers holding work permits have the same legal status as their German colleagues.

## Worker Participation

Germany has moved, more than most societies in the free world, in the direction of worker participation. The Shop Organization Act of 1972, which applies to all businesses employing five or more persons, provides a variety of rights of codetermination both in social and personnel questions.

For example, in large companies with five hundred or more employees, one-third of the directors must be representatives of the employees (except in the coal and steel industries, where half the supervisory board must be employees). In addition, even in small firms there is a Works Council, which further represents the interests of the workers vis-à-vis the employer.

As one might expect, trade unions are strong in Germany. About seven million workers are members of the largest one, the German Union Federation (*Deutscher Gewerkschaftsbund* or DGB), which actually comprises sixteen individual trade unions. The salaried, white-collar technical and public service employees have professional associations of their own, such as the German Civil Servants Association (*Beamtenbund*), German Salaried Employees Union (*Deutsche Angestellten-Gewerkschaft* or DAG), and the German Armed Forces Association (*Bundeswehrverband*). Trade unions and employer associations negotiate agreements on working conditions without the involvement of the state. Usually, they are successful in their efforts; however, the workers' right to strike and the employers' right to lockout are available as ultimate expedients. Basically, these rights of protest (union) and self-protection (employers) encourage negotiation and are the foundation of the harmonious labor-management-government relations. This balance of cooperation and autonomy is also the basis for Germany's extremely high productivity and for the strength of the agreements made between labor and management.

## CHURCHES AND RELIGION

To those who are accustomed to and believe strongly in the separation of church and state, the system in Germany may come as a surprise. Churches in Germany are supported by an 8-10 percent tax on income. This tax is collected by the internal revenue office and distributed to two church administrations: the *Evangelische Landeskirche*, composed of Lutheran and Evangelical churches, and the Catholic Church.

The funds are used to maintain and construct church buildings, compensate the clergy, and support religious observances. The funds are also used to operate institutions such as hospitals, nursing homes, schools, kindergartens, and day-care centers. Smaller groups, including the Baptists (*Freie Kirche*), Methodists, and Jehovah's Witnesses receive support from voluntary, tax-exempt contributions of members. Members of other religious groups, atheists, and those who have officially dropped their church affiliation are not required to pay the church tax.

Christianity as a religious preference predominates in the Federal Republic; about 49 percent of the population are Protestant; almost 45 percent are Roman Catholic. Less than 1 percent are Jewish. About 40 percent attend church regularly. Protestantism tends to be stronger in the north and Catholicism dominates in parts of the Rhineland and in the south.

Because so many state-related services involve the church, connections with the church are useful if you wish to function in German society and make social connections. Each parish contains roughly 3,500 people, and the pastor has specific duties to carry out within his or her parish and may be involved in activities ranging from organizing and leading tours and teaching religion in the schools to conducting weddings and funeral services and visiting the sick. Pastors are engaged in the secular and ceremonial life of the community to a remarkable degree. Courses in religion are taught in the schools, but parents may request that their child be exempted from religious instruction. Children over the age of fourteen can decide to eliminate religion from their course of study.

# 2

# Before Leaving

## REGULATIONS

For entry into the Federal Republic a U.S. citizen (and many other nationalities as well) needs a passport but not a visa; nor are immunizations required in many cases. Nevertheless, you may want to obtain an international health record card on which to keep personal health information.

Foreigners planning to stay more than three months must obtain permits: a work permit for anyone who is employed and a residence permit for each member of the family, even an infant. This residence permit or *Aufenthaltserlaubnis* will be documented in your passport. Although it is best to get this permit in advance through a German consulate, it is possible to obtain one in Germany if you file for it within three months after arrival at the alien department (*Ausländeramt*) in the city or county administration offices nearest to you. Residence permits are granted only if you have proof that the work permit is or will be granted.

You must obtain the work permit, or *Arbeitserlaubnis*, before you begin working in Germany. Often you will receive it along with the residence permit, but if not (often the case with a spouse who decides to work after arrival), you can apply for it at the local employment office (*Arbeitsamt*).

Within a week after your arrival in the Federal Republic, you must register with the community or mayor's office of your locality. Hotels do this for their guests, which is why they usually collect your passport when you check in and keep it overnight. When you rent a house or an apartment, you must complete the same registration form, and when vacating your living quarters, you must file a report within one week. You will also need a Tax Card, which is obtained from the district tax office.

This may seem like a lot of paperwork and red tape, and you may find it irritating at times if you are not used to it. Germany is simply a thorough, deliberate, and careful society; as a guest, it is necessary to live within the system.

## CUSTOMS REGULATIONS

When entering the Federal Republic, individuals may take the following items duty-free, but they must be hand-carried or in accompanying luggage (they should not be shipped with household goods). All items should be for personal use only.

- Gifts worth up to DM 100.00 (easiest if these are hand-carried)
- Four hundred cigarettes or 100 cigars or one pound of tobacco
- One quart of liquor
- Eight ounces of coffee or three ounces of powdered coffee or an even smaller amount of tea
- One pint of eau de cologne and 1.7 ounces of perfume

Smokers will probably want to take their limit; tobacco prices are high.

### Import of Household Goods

Household goods may be imported into Germany without payment of customs duty or border tax on presentation to the German customs authorities of reasonable proof of the following:

1.  You have given up your previous residence abroad (e.g., documents showing the termination of your lease and/ or employment or the sale of your residential house); or you have been transferred to Germany by your employer. Maintaining two residences (that is, keeping your residence at home) does not necessarily result in a denial of customs exemption if you are also establishing a new German residence.

2.  You are establishing a residence in Germany (i.e., a lease, correspondence with your employer, German police registration receipt.

Customs exemption is granted **only** for goods that you have been using personally or professionally abroad and which you intend to use again in Germany. Food and similar perishable items are restricted to quantities normally stored at home. Liquor and tobacco products are not permitted duty-free except for the amount you are allowed to carry with you when entering the country (see page 15).

A motor vehicle that was registered in your name(s) as the sole owner(s) at your previous place of residence may also be imported to Germany duty-free, provided you have a registration certificate from your previous motor vehicles registry authority. Although there is no minimum requirement for the length of time of your ownership, German customs must be satisfied that you are importing it for personal use only.

Before they can be licensed, cars must pass inspection by the German Technical Inspection Team, and cars of foreign manufacture may have to undergo certain modifications to conform to existing German requirements. Since this can be rather expensive, it is usually less costly to bring in only relatively new cars (for more information on import or purchase of cars, see chapter 9).

All household goods should arrive at approximately the same time you arrive in Germany. If that is impossible, the goods should arrive as soon as possible after you enter the country. If you declare personal belongings on arrival, you will have a three-year time limit for receiving the goods. A detailed description of the contents of your shipment must be presented to customs officials when you arrive, even if your shipment will not be arriving for many months.

This information is included only as a general guide. The German Customs Office will ascertain whether the effects to be imported are reasonably consistent with your personal, professional, and economic status. Special rules govern items such as guns, rifles, ammunition and machines used to produce them, certain pets, and plants. More detailed information can be obtained from the nearest German consulate or from the German Embassy.

When you leave Germany, you may export your household goods freely, with no limitations on food, alcoholic beverages, or tobacco products. You need, however, to be concerned about the regulations at your next destination.

## Importing Pets

Germans are pet lovers, so if you decide to take your pet(s), you will have a minimum of difficulty. Dogs, if well behaved, can usually be taken on trains (an extra fee is charged on first-class trains) and are often permitted in hotels and even restaurants. Vets are excellent, and you will find every kind of food and equipment for almost any animal or bird.

If you bring a dog or cat into Germany, you must have the animal vaccinated against rabies within ten days prior to your entering the country, and you must also present a notarized German translation of the vaccination certificate. In addition you must provide a health certificate or a letter written on the veterinarian's stationery stating that the animal is in good health. This letter or certificate must be written in German or accompanied by a translation, and it must (1) state the name, breed, color, sex, and age of the animal,

(2) be prepared at the point of origin within ten days of the pet's arrival date, and (3) attest to the nonoccurrence of rabies within a thirteen-mile radius of the pet's home within the past three months. For your own protection, have your pet inoculated for all possible diseases. If your pet regularly takes any medication, you should carry a supply with you, along with a letter from the veterinarian naming the medication and describing the reason for its use.

Arrangements for your pet's transportation should be made with the airline as far in advance as possible because the number of animals the airline can carry on a flight is limited. Most airlines, with sufficient notice, will provide an appropriate animal carrier. Lufthansa and KLM have particularly good "Jet-Pet" service. If you provide you own carrier, make sure it is approved by the airline prior to your departure. Also, check with your vet for medication (relaxant or tranquilizer) which will make the trip easier for your pet.

## WHAT TO TAKE

Although Germans are becoming increasingly casual in dress, they are generally quite concerned about dressing appropriately. Throughout Europe, people dress well in public and would not, for example, wear shorts or bright sportswear on city streets.

Germany's cool climate dictates your wardrobe to a large degree. Winters are cold and damp; in the north the wind blows off the sea and the fog rolls in frequently. Even in the summer, it seldom gets excessively hot, so generally warm clothing is recommended. Bring windproof jackets, pile-lined or down coats, and warm nightwear since houses are often chilly. Sturdy rainwear (raincoats with zip-out linings are handy) and boots are necessities.

Men will need the usual business clothing: suits, shirts, and ties of the same weight as would be appropriate in most cold climates. Sports clothes will be useful as well. Both men and women should take a good supply of shoes since German shoes are sized differently, making it hard to find shoes that fit. If you are able to find a fit, you will find that German shoes are well made and quite reasonably priced. Be sure to bring sturdy walking shoes for the cobblestone streets and for sightseeing.

Women wear wool most of the year—suits, wool dresses or slacks (which are worn a great deal), warm hats, and a winter coat. Take stockings and underwear since they, like shoes, are sized differently. Also, bring one or two cocktail dresses and possibly a long dress since German social occasions are often quite formal.

In comparison to adults, young people tend to dress very casually. Children and teens wear blue jeans and T-shirts. You will notice that many teenage girls wear small purses around their necks (not over the shoulder) because they are convenient and less likely to be lost or snatched. Clothes of all kinds are available for young people and for infants and children, as are cloth and disposable diapers.

You can buy almost any type of clothing you might want or need. High-priced coats and suits are excellent and well styled, but medium-priced clothing, although well made, tends to be designed more for German tastes.

For information on household appliances, see chapter 6.

# 3

# On Arrival

## MONEY MATTERS

### Currency

The monetary unit in Germany is the *Deutschemark* (DM), which is divided into one hundred *Pfennigs*.

Notes: DM 5, 10, 20, 50, 100, 500, 1000
Coins: Pfennigs 1, 2, 5 (rare nowadays), 10, 50; DM 1, 2, 5

Learning a new currency system takes time, so it is a good idea before you leave home to get a packet of German money through your bank or a money exchange office. You and your family can practice and become comfortable with the bills and coins and their values, and you will have one less thing to adjust to when you first arrive. Having a supply of German coins and small bills will make tipping porters and paying taxis on arrival much less confusing. If you are unable to get German money prior to your departure, the flight attendant may be able to change a small amount.

A currency exchange office (*Geldwechsel* or *Wechselstube*) or a bank can be found at most airports and major railway stations. Currency exchange offices are numerous and are sometimes open past regular banking hours. You can, of course, exchange money at a hotel, but you will generally receive a lower rate of exchange.

Germany has no currency restrictions either incoming or outgoing, but the U.S. does. You must file a report with U.S. customs if you depart from or return to the U.S. with more than $5,000 in cash, foreign currency, traveler's checks, money orders, or any negotiable funds. The same applies to money mailed to or from the U.S.

Almost everything in Germany is expensive, especially housing. Shopping at the weekly markets is a good way to save on fruits, vegetables, and flowers as well as to insure that you are purchasing the freshest produce. Also, look for local beers and wines, for which Germany is famous. Since Germany belongs to the Common Market, there are no high import tariffs on goods from other member nations.

Naturally, the cost of living changes and prices fluctuate. How expensive it will seem to you depends on where you have lived before. Prices are more or less comparable to those in New York City, Washington, DC, or San Francisco.

## Banking and Credit Cards

Opening a German bank account is a wise move. One reason is convenience: it is not easy to get personal foreign checks cashed in business places or hotels. You can cash U.S. checks at the First National Bank, Chase Bank, Bank of America, and American Express in the bigger cities, but German banks and American Express charge a fee for cashing foreign bank checks. Getting a local German check cashed, however, is quite easy. You can also have regular bills (such as rent, phone, etc.) paid by bank transfer orders. You might want to investigate this system, particularly if you are out of the country frequently. German banks do not return canceled checks or provide monthly statements, so keeping accurate records is important.

Another alternative is opening a Postal Savings Account at the post office, where you not only can pay most bills for only a few Pfennigs but can also open a savings account. Inquire about this on arrival.

Credit cards are not widely accepted. Several international credit cards (including the useful Eurocredit card, which is similar to MasterCard or Visa but is issued by European banks and payable in local currency) are accepted in hotels, airlines, major shops, and some restaurants, but in most places you will need cash. If you are planning to use American Express or other U.S. cards, advise the company of your new address in Germany. This will help you avoid late payment penalties because of a delay in the arrival of your bill.

## Taxes

Individuals registered as permanent residents of Germany are taxed on all income and benefits from sources both inside and outside of Germany. However, under double taxation conventions, your income will not be fully taxed by both your home and the German governments. Those not permanently residing in the Federal Republic are subject only to limited income tax on the income acquired there.

Tax rates are steeply progressive and cover indirect as well as direct benefits (i.e., employer contributions to pension plans, etc.). Narrowly defined deductions are allowed for "expenditures to create, protect or preserve income." Foreigners may request a special "lump sum deduction" called a *Pauschalierung*. If you are a U.S. citizen, you may find it desirable to send for the government booklet "Tax Guide for U.S. Citizens Abroad," updated annually and available free from the district IRS office or from IRS, Washington, DC 20225. A pamphlet by Price Waterhouse, "Information for Doing Business in West Germany," also contains a great deal of helpful information and is available on request from Price Waterhouse, 1251 Avenue of the Americas, New York, NY 10020.

Automobiles are subject to a tax based on cylinder capacity; there are also minimal annual taxes on radios and television sets.

Value added tax, or VAT, is a tax on the increase in the price of goods and services that occurs at each step of production or performance—the "value added" at each stage. It is similar to sales tax but is levied by the national government rather than at the local level and so is the same throughout the country.

Tax laws are complex; be sure to get good tax advice before you leave for Germany. If you need additional assistance in-country and your employer is unable to provide it, your embassy will usually help. There is an IRS office at the U.S. Embassy in Bonn, and several "Big 8" accounting firms have offices in Germany.

## Tipping

Tipping is customary in the FRG and the following guidelines will generally apply:

- Hotels and restaurants: a 10-15 percent service charge is added to your bill (in addition to the VAT)

- Porters: DM 2 per bag

- Hotel maids: DM 2-5 per night

- Taxi drivers: 10 percent of the fare

- Cloakroom attendants: small change

- Hairdresser: 10-15 percent of the total charge

- Hotel concierge: for special services (amount depends on the service supplied)

- Movie and theater ushers: no tip expected

In general, special services should be rewarded.

## USEFUL INFORMATION

Germany is one hour ahead of Greenwich Mean Time (GMT), London, and six hours ahead of Eastern Standard Time (EST), New York. Daylight Savings Time is in effect between late March and late September. The dates vary but are announced in advance in all local papers.

As is true all over Europe, Germans use the international time system, with the twenty-four hour clock (8:00 P.M. is 2000; 9:30 P.M. is 2130).

## Business Hours

Most business offices are usually open from 0830 to 1700, but factories generally start earlier. As in most cities, the streets are filled with traffic by 0700.

Banking hours are from 0830 to 1230 or 1300 and from 1430 to 1600, Monday through Friday, except for Thursdays, when banks close at 1730.

Stores are open from 0800 or 0900 to about 1830 on weekdays; they close on Saturdays at 1400 except on the first Saturday of each month, when shops stay open until 1800 or 1830. In many outlying districts and rural villages, the 1300-1500 "siesta closing" is still practiced.

Post offices (*Postämter*) are open from 0800 until noon and again from 1400 to 1730; they close at noon on Saturdays. (German public mailboxes are yellow.)

Government offices are usually open from 0830 to 1730 during the week and are closed on Saturdays.

Drugstores (*Apotheken*) generally observe shop hours and will display a special sign if they are open all night and on Sundays.

## Public Holidays

Businesses normally close on the following public holidays:

| | |
|---|---|
| January 1 | New Year's Day |
| March/April (dates vary) | Good Friday and Easter Monday |
| May 1 | Labor Day |
| May (date varies) | Ascension Day |
| May/June (varies) | Whit Monday |
| June (varies) | Corpus Christi Day (Catholic areas) |

| | |
|---|---|
| June 17 | German Unity or Berlin Day |
| November 1 | All Saints' Day (Catholic areas) |
| November (varies) | Repentance Day |
| December 25 | Christmas Day |
| December 26 | Second Day of Christmas |

Business slows down between June 1 and August 30 (it seems all of Europe is on vacation in August) as well as before and after the Christmas and Easter holidays.

## Dates and Numbers

The German system of writing dates may be confusing at first; for example, 6/7/89 means the sixth of July 1989, not the seventh of June. This system, used throughout Europe, is quite logical: the day, the month, and then the year.

In Europe and Britain, numbers are written in a way that may be unfamiliar to you. A horizontal line is drawn through the leg of the number seven so that it looks a bit like a reversed $F$ ($\not{7}$); this differentiates it from the one, which often looks quite like an American seven ($7$). If you want to indicate a number on your fingers, you should start counting from your thumb (thumb for one, thumb and index finger for two, etc.). The period and comma are used differently as well. A period separates billions, millions, thousands, and hundreds; the comma only sets off the decimal fraction, for example, 100.290,55.

## TRANSPORTATION

Transportation is modern and very efficient in Germany. Railroads and highways are excellent, and the network of navigable rivers and canals carries a great volume of freight (all railways, airports and seaports, and major bus lines are government owned). Rental cars are available and taxi services are good. Getting around should not be difficult.

## Transportation in Cities

**Taxis**. Fares vary from city to city and are based on time, zones, and distances. You will be charged an extra fee for each suitcase and, if it applies, for your dog. You can order cabs by phone for a small surcharge or pick them up at taxi stands. Although tipping is not compulsory, most people tip the driver about DM 1 or 2 for fares up to DM 10 and about 10 percent for higher fares.

**Trams, Buses, and Subways**. Public transportation is clean, quick, efficient, and plentiful and is a good way to see a new city as well as to get around efficiently and inexpensively. Purchase bus and tram tickets from the conductor or from a ticket dispenser, or sometimes from the driver. In the larger cities, you can purchase a booklet of tickets if you use the bus or tram regularly. The bus stop sign (*Bushaltestelle*) is easy to see; in some places you may see *Bedarfshaltestelle*, (stop on request). Unless someone is waiting at the stop and signals the bus driver, the bus will not stop.

Subways, or the underground *U-Bahn*, operate in Berlin, Hamburg, Frankfurt, München, Bonn, and Düsseldorf, providing an excellent means of transportation. Lines extend into the suburbs from the city centers, and the fare is the same, no matter how far you travel. Also, if you use this service regularly, purchase a book of tickets which gives you a small savings over the individual fares. The subways do not run between 0100 and 0500.

**Trains**. One of the joys of traveling in Europe is riding the trains, and the German railroad system is among the best. Trains are fast, comfortable, and reliable though not always frequent. Long-distance trains are especially pleasant. As a train leaves a station, the conductor will announce the next stop. Be ready to get off the trains the minute they stop, as they often stay in the stations only a brief time. Arrivals and departures are not normally announced inside the stations; one watches for the predicted time of arrival and for station signs. There are a number of different types of trains:

- Personenzug: local train, stops at all stations
- E-Zug: stops often but not at every station

- D-Zug: express train
- IC-Zug: intercity express (sometimes carries multilingual secretaries as a service to businesspeople)
- T.E.E.: Trans-European Express (first class only, reservation required)

**Air Service**. Frankfurt is Germany's most active international airport and air transport hub. There are international facilities in most major cities as well, but flights will generally make a stop in Frankfurt. Additionally, there are frequent flights between the major cities. Lufthansa, the German national airline, is known for its fine service. Of course, all major international airlines service the Federal Republic (see chapter 11 for information on specific cities).

## COMMUNICATIONS

## The Telephone System

Public phones, which are owned by the postal system, are bright yellow in color and are not as numerous as you might expect. Because the system is fully automated, you cannot make any operator-assisted calls from these phones. To make a collect or credit-card call, you must use your own phone or go to the post office.

There are two types of phones in each booth: the *Telephon* or *Ortsgespräche* for local calls only (no time limit), and the *Ferngespräche* for local and long-distance calls. You can dial any long-distance call within the republic by depositing several coins before dialing. Unused coins will be returned automatically at the end of your call.

Rates are reduced after 1800 and on weekends, with the lowest rate (night rate) applying between 2200 and 0600 daily and all day Saturday, Sunday, and holidays. Collect calls can be made to the U.S. at the person-to-person rate. Try to avoid charging long-distance calls on your hotel bill because the surcharges can be extremely high. For information on obtaining a phone in your house/apartment, see chapter 6.

The Yellow Pages (*Gelbe Seiten*) contain essentially the same type of information as they do elsewhere. On page 1 you find emergency numbers and listings for directory assistance, repair service, telegram service, time, weather, and other information services. Current postal rates are listed on page 3. Listings are arranged alphabetically and there is an index at the end of the book. If you find a "Q" next to the phone number, that means the phone will be answered by a recording. Free copies are available at your post office if there is no copy in your house or apartment.

The White Pages provide personal and business phone numbers and addresses arranged in alphabetical order. Area codes (*Vorwahlen*) are listed in a small yellow book that comes with the White Pages. These are generally posted above the phone in public phone booths as well.

## Postal Service

The postal service, like most of the transportation system, is owned by the government and is excellent. Mail is delivered once a day—in the morning. Stamps are available at post offices or hotels.

The Federal Republic (and West Berlin) has been divided into eight main postal districts. The biggest city in each district has a one-digit postal number (1 Berlin, 2 Hamburg, etc.) and towns within that district have 2, 3, or 4 numbers according to size. Frankfurt, for example, is 6; Wiesbaden, being smaller but in the Frankfurt postal district, is 62; Idstein, a smaller town near Wiesbaden and within its subdistrict, is 627; a little village outside Idstein is 6271.

The logic in addressing envelopes German-fashion is to proceed in order of importance—first the name of the addressee, on the next line the zip code number and name of the city or town, then the name of the street and the house number. Underline the town or city and put the zip code to the left.

The post office handles telegrams, telephone and telex services, and collects radio and TV fees. It also offers a banking service, with both savings and checking accounts, and a subscription service for newspapers and magazines. Cables can be sent from private phones or from the post office. It also pays out social security and other federal pensions and has a fleet of post buses which carry passengers.

Telex service is part of the postal system and is widely used in Germany; you can set up charge or credit arrangements. Telex service is also often available in hotels, at trade fairs, etc.

## Radio and TV

Although Germany has nine radio stations, most local programming originates from either Hamburg or Köln, the two large regional stations. A wide variety of programs, including extensive news coverage, is available. English-language programs are also broadcast by BBC, Radio Luxembourg, and the American Armed Forces in Germany. Radio Stuttgart carries many English-language broadcasts as well, including facts and information about Germany, the people, and their lives. It also broadcasts practical information about the weather, road conditions, and current activities. The American radio station "RIAS" beams programs to the Soviet Union from West Berlin. With proper equipment, you can pick up these broadcasts throughout Germany and in other European countries.

A shortwave radio is welcome because it helps you keep up with sports, music, and news from home. It also gives you access to music from Moscow and La Scala or the great festivals of Salzburg or Edinburgh and permits some "eavesdropping" on the Voice of America and Radio Free Europe.

There are two government-operated TV networks (called *Programmes* in Germany) and a third regional network which operates daily, broadcasting plays, opera, news, etc. A small monthly tax on both TV and radio sets provides the Programmes with operating funds and allows them greater independence since they don't have to rely on advertising (of which there is very little) for operating income. Although state-owned stations are independent, they are supervised by a nongovernment civil authority.

## Publications

This highly literate nation has 1,250 daily newspapers and about 9,400 periodicals, all privately owned. *Das Bild*, published in Hamburg, is the largest and most influential German-language newspaper, with a circulation of nearly five million. *Der Spiegel*, also published in Hamburg, is the German equivalent of *Time* or *Newsweek*. The German Press Agency (DPA—*Deutsche Presse Agentur*) is the leading news service, with offices all over the world.

## English-Language Publications

Major U.S. and other international papers and magazines are available one to three weeks after publication. The *International Herald Tribune* is available on a current daily basis, as are the U.S. Army's *Stars and Stripes* and British and French newspapers. The European or international editions of *Time* and *Newsweek* are available on the date of issue. The larger bookstores carry limited selections of books in English, and some English-language paperbacks are available in train stations and airports as well. Unfortunately, though, books are very expensive.

The *German Tribune* is an English-language weekly that summarizes major stories that have appeared in the German press; it can be ordered from the *German Tribune*, Friedrich Reinecke Verlag GmbH, D-2000 Hamburg 76, 23 Schöne Aussicht, Federal Republic of Germany.

*Aussenpolitik*, a quarterly foreign affairs review, is available in an English edition; the publisher will send a sample copy at no obligation. It can be ordered from Interpress GmbH, D-2000 Hamburg 76, Holsteinischer Kamp 14, Federal Republic of Germany.

## LANGUAGE

To get the most out of your stay in Germany, try your hardest to learn German. While you will find that many Germans do speak English and that you can get along without learning German, you will greatly increase your enjoyment and understanding of Germany and the German people if you can speak the language. Even if your German is far from perfect, people will respect you and respond warmly to your efforts.

One of the most important German words for you to know and use is *bitte*. Bitte (bit' tah) is the word for both "please" and "you are welcome." To acknowledge an apology, reply *"bitte schön"* or *"bitte sehr,"* meaning essentially "don't mention it." When you hold a door open for someone, pick up something that has fallen, hand someone a forgotten paper—any small courtesy—accompany it with a smile, a nod, and the word *bitte*. When you are offered seconds on food in a German home or restaurant, "bitte," or "ja, bitte" (ya bit' tah) indicates acceptance.

If you want to say "no, thank you," you may, depending on the context, simply use the word *danke* (dahng' kah), or *nein, danke* (nine' dahng kah).

There are two ways to say "excuse me," each with a different meaning. If you step on or bump into someone and want to excuse yourself, you say *Verzeihung, wie bitte?* (fehr tsigh' ung vee bit' tah), "forgive or pardon me please." This same phrase also means "I beg your pardon." If, however, you want to ask if you may pass or get by someone, you say *gestatten sie* (ge shtah' ten zee) *bitte*, which means "please permit me." More commonly used is simply *pardon*, with the accent on the second syllable.

People tend to greet each other with some vigor, so a hearty *Guten Morgen* (goo' ten mor' gen)—or whatever greeting is appropriate for the time of day—should be used. When departing, a sincere *Auf Wiedersehen* (owf vee' der zey en) is appreciated.

Schools and institutes teaching German have multiplied in all major German cities. Consult the Yellow Pages of your local phone book. Embassies, consulates, churches, and clubs can provide additional leads. You can also get a private tutor or a student to come to supper certain nights a week and help the family with the language. Another alternative is simply to put yourselves in German-speaking environments where you will have to listen and speak in German.

Another good way to pick up German is to attend German movies and to listen to German on radio and TV. Even if you do not understand what is being said, your ears are becoming accustomed to the language, and before long you will be able to pick out single words, then phrases, then the main idea of the program. Children's television shows can also be a useful learning tool.

When you shop, pay attention to labels—read everything. It will help you add useful nouns and verbs to your vocabulary as well as make your shopping more efficient in the long run. Frequent the small local shops for your groceries and learn how to place your order in German. After a while you will be able to carry on a simple conversation with the shopkeepers. If you are a loyal customer, the shopkeepers will be quite willing to talk and put up with your broken German. Just don't be afraid to use your new vocabulary. You'll both be able to have a good laugh over your faux pas in German.

Children or older people in your neighborhood can also be good helpers. Both groups always seem to have enough time to chat and are interested in sharing information with newcomers.

In short, use as many methods to learn German as you can, particularly those fitted to your particular style of learning. And use German as often as you can.

# 4

# Values and Customs

Two words which underlie most German social customs are *reserve* and *formality*, and both are expressed in a number of ways. While the attitudes and behaviors discussed in this section will not be true for everyone, they will provide a broad framework within which some of the reactions of the Germans can be understood.

These quotes are some general comparisons made by Germans familiar with Americans:

"You delight in being occupied. We believe in contemplation."

"You say, 'business before pleasure.' We close our store and go on vacation."

"You are accustomed to new programs and schedules. Frequent change bothers us."

"You sell your home and move into a new one. We are the third generation to live in ours."

"You admire movie stars and athletes. We admire professors."

"You dye your hair and watch your weight to retain a youthful appearance. We let nature take its course."

"You pursue happiness. We are content with good health."

"You believe in sharing everything almost immediately: your

thoughts, your feelings, your possessions. We are more careful in our choices of those whom we trust, whom we love and share things with."

## CONSCIENTIOUSNESS

A job well done is something to be proud of, and doing things well and thoroughly is very important to the conscientious German. The German housewife considers herself to be the best housekeeper in the world and resents being told how to do things more efficiently or more economically. She is slow to change and considers an idea a long time before adopting it. And doing a job well doesn't mean that it is done fast. Don't expect a twenty-four-hour rush job from the cleaners (or anyone). Careful thought and planning go into anything that is efficient, worthwhile, and respectable. For a German there is no such thing as learning a trade or business by trial and error. One should learn it at school or in a training program, no matter how long it takes. (This also applies to language learning!)

## RESPECT FOR THE INTELLECTUAL

Intelligence is a German's most valuable asset, and gaining knowledge is not an individual endeavor; the state pays for education. Germans praise ideas rather than deeds and admire the well-educated intellectual who can think and reason, whether his or her ideas are implemented or not. Action is not as important as the idea behind it. A German's list of most admired persons would generally be headed by a professor, even though professors produce no marketable "product."

Intelligence is demonstrated in many ways: a broad education, social grace, speaking and spelling correctly. To be ignorant of something is degrading to a German—quite different from the American attitude that a lack of knowledge is all right as long as you admit to it.

Conversely, the American admires the kind of intelligence that can be used to create practical results or convert ideas into products. Americans like to see results and don't especially care if the person producing them has obtained an advanced education. In fact those who have succeeded without the benefit of formal study are frequently admired for their achievement.

## PRIVACY

The German need for privacy manifests itself in numerous ways, some of which are also found elsewhere in northern Europe. Office doors, and doors in general, are usually closed in Germany. Fences and large gates surround dwellings throughout Europe. The need for privacy has its roots in Europe's violent history and also in the sheer density of population. Europeans are not accustomed to the wide open spaces that have shaped American culture. Because of these historical influences, European tradition leans toward mistrusting a stranger rather than welcoming him or her and toward clearly defining personal space rather than allowing the boundaries to be ambiguous.

## FORMALITY

The German may strike you as being cold and formal, but you should not interpret this formality as avoidance. It is rather an expression of respect. To the American, the better you know someone, the more casual you can be with that person. The German feels that bonds should be built on respect rather than on casualness.

Social prestige is determined in large measure by profession. While wealth, family history, and land ownership play a role in conferring status, education and individual achievement are perceived as the key to social standing. Thus, titles earned from intellectual effort are important. Germans address each other (with only few exceptions) using *Herr*, *Frau*, or *Fraulein*, followed by either title, family name, or both, for example: Herr *Doktor* Schmidt (for both medical and academic doctors) or Herr *Professor*, with or without a name. You may hear people addressed with multiple honorifics ("Herr Professor *Advocat*") as a further acknowledgement of multiple degrees or professions. A useful term which fits the head of any business, government office, hotel, or the like is *Direktor*. If you do not know someone's name but do know his or her occupation, you can feel comfortable using the title only, for example, Herr or Frau Doktor or Herr/Frau Direktor. First names are normally used only by family members or very close acquaintances or friends. Do not address someone by his or her first name unless asked to do so.

*Gnädige Frau* is the most polite form of address; it conveys respect and is appropriate when greeting older or high-ranking women. If you don't know someone's name, you can simply address a woman as Frau and a man as Herr. A woman may be addressed by her own first name (not her husband's, e.g., Frau Gerda Maier, not Frau Hans Maier) but is generally addressed by her husband's title (Frau Doktor Maier). When addressing envelopes, use Herr or Frau plus the title and name, for example, Frau Dr. (usually abbreviated) Gerda Maier or Frau Gerda Maier. When addressing an envelope to both husband and wife, use Herr Hans Maier und Frau.

Young Germans are less title-conscious than the older generation, as are those who have mixed a great deal with people from other countries. Young people use *Du* (informal "you") easily with their peers; this informality is also common among manual laborers. Office colleagues, however, normally use *Sie* (the formal, polite "you"), as do people you meet in most other situations. As with first names, do not use Du unless asked to do so. These language rules don't apply when using English, of course, but other ways of expressing informality and familiarity should be avoided until the relationship has developed to a point where a closeness and greater familiarity are appropriate. As in almost everything, let the host be the leader.

# HANDSHAKING

The German form of greeting is the handshake, not a smile. Smiles are a sign of friendship. (People aren't being unfriendly when they don't smile. They don't know you, so how can they feel a connection with you?) People in Europe, and especially Germans, shake hands constantly in both formal and informal situations, with friends as well as with acquaintances or strangers. If you stop to chat with someone on the street, you shake hands on meeting and on bidding farewell. When you enter the office and again before you leave at night, you shake hands with all your close colleagues. At small social gatherings, you shake hands with everyone on arrival (while stating your last name) and again on departure. At large parties, shaking hands with those to whom you are introduced is appropriate.

Following this ritual is often difficult for newcomers (especially the departing handshake, which is readily forgotten), but the impression you give (or do not give) makes this social convention well worth practicing until you can do it without thinking or feeling self-conscious. The German handshake is firm, but not hard, and more of a "clasping" than a "pumping" gesture. And also worthy of note, the woman offers her hand for shaking before the man.

The German "hand kiss" occurs in the air slightly above the hand. It is given only to married women or ladies of great esteem, and never outdoors. This is a practice not recommended to foreign men because it is a delicate, culturally rooted custom with which many foreigners are neither familiar nor comfortable. Women should not be startled, however, when German men make the gesture.


# MANNERS

To Americans good manners are an indication of a good upbringing. To Germans good manners are a necessity for everyone, regardless of background or education. Germans realize that you are a foreigner and do not expect you to know about their customs, but poor manners will get you off to a bad start, which will be difficult if not impossible to compensate for at a later time. Good manners will be recognized and appreciated, so a bit of time spent in practicing will be a valuable investment.

Children are taught from an early age how to behave and are expected to exhibit proper manners at all times. Boys are expected to make a slight bow when greeting an adult, and all children are taught to greet adults with a handshake and a good, strong greeting: "Guten Morgen, Herr Schmidt," looking them straight in the eye. Teaching your children these small courtesies will go far in insuring that they are accepted. American children, in particular, are considered to be quite rude, mostly because they tend to interrupt and fail to greet visiting adults properly.

On the theory that the escort goes ahead to make sure everything is all right, men precede women through doors and into public places such as restaurants, and theaters (and down theater aisles). Since this is the opposite of the "ladies first" custom in the U.S., it seems odd to Americans and warrants mention.

As a basic rule, a man walks on the left side of a woman in Germany, in the streets and elsewhere. The right side is the "place of honor," so to speak. (Therefore, a young girl will always walk on the left side of an older woman.) The custom behind this is very old, originating in the Middle Ages when the gentleman would walk on the left so that he could draw his sword quickly and easily for the protection of his companion. However, when you are walking along a very narrow street, through heavy traffic, or along a dirty gutter, then the man walks on the side of the traffic (danger).

Men may or may not take a woman's arm when escorting her. Women shouldn't be surprised if a German woman acquaintance links arms with them while they are walking along the street. It is quite proper, quite common, and once you get used to it, quite a pleasant custom as well as a sign of friendship.

# TIME: PROMPTNESS

Right on time, neither too early nor too late—that's the German attitude towards time. Being prompt when arriving at any appointment (business or social) is very important. If you are more than ten minutes late, a very good excuse is expected, along with apologies. To be as much as thirty minutes late is simply unacceptable, so if you are unavoidably detained, it is best to call as soon as possible and explain. When the time for an official or academic function is listed with the abbreviation "c.t." (*con tempore*), it will begin promptly at fifteen minutes after the hour. If "s.t." (*sine tempore*) is given, the function begins on the hour.

Although punctuality is paramount, the Germans don't live the fast pace of life that is often associated with time consciousness. They prefer a slower lifestyle and do not think, as Americans do, that "time is money."

# FRIENDSHIP

The Germans make a clear distinction between *ein Freund* (a friend) and *ein Bekannte* (an acquaintance). One may have a close acquaintance for many years and still not consider the person to be ein Freund. Even the use of the Du form doesn't necessarily indicate that one is a friend. Ein Freund indicates a person with whom you spend a lot of time, with whom you share interests, and whom you would expect to help in any emergency. In other words, a friend is someone to whom you would give "the shirt off your back"—and more.

The words *Du* and *Freund*, then, are only used to indicate very special relationships, more like a "close or dear friend" in the U.S. It takes a long time for a friendship to develop because it requires that a lot of attention, interest, and even financial assistance (if needed) be given to the other person. Since Germans do not move from place to place very much, friends are generally close geographically as well as emotionally. Because of the strong commitment involved, it is understandable that people are cautious about becoming involved. Once this lifetime commitment is made, the ensuing relationship is very close, extremely rewarding, highly valued, and potentially demanding.

## SOCIAL CUSTOMS

**Invitations.** If you say to a German, even a casual acquaintance, that you would "like to get together some day," you will be taken literally. Your acquaintance will expect a specific invitation, and if it is not forthcoming, the omission will be considered poor manners on your part.

If you must refuse an invitation, any reasonable excuse is acceptable. Only sickness and official business are valid excuses when canceling an engagement, however, and the hosts should be notified as soon as possible.

When you are invited to someone's home for the first time, it is customary to take some flowers or chocolates to the hostess. If you should forget, it is acceptable to send them afterwards with a thank-you note. A florist can suggest the appropriate flowers. You should purchase an odd number of flowers (3,5,7, etc.) to indicate that you don't want this visit to be the last one. Since red roses mean love, they do not make a good hostess gift under ordinary circumstances. Mums should also be avoided as they are associated with funerals. Before giving the flowers to your hostess, you should remove all wrapping except cellophane from around them.

If a party is likely to be large, or if it is being given in your honor, send flowers in advance with a note stating how much you are looking forward to the evening.

The host and hostess usually greet guests at the door, shake hands, and help them with their coats (see information on handshaking above). When two couples greet each other, the women shake hands first. When a German guest arrives at your home for any event, no matter how simple, he or she will almost invariably say "thank you for your invitation." It is courteous for you to do the same when arriving at a German home.

Strangers do not introduce themselves if the hostess is busy; they wait to be introduced. Women do not stand when being introduced unless it is to someone much older than themselves or someone of high rank.

Europeans feel that hard liquor and smoking both dull the taste buds and prevent the enjoyment of fine food, so there is no smoking during a meal, and the cocktail hour before a meal is short (all the more reason to be prompt). Wine and beer are served during the meal, and cigarettes (perhaps with brandy) may be offered after coffee.

All in all, German hosts tend to be very gracious; they expend every effort to make their guests welcome and to insure an enjoyable evening. There are so few rules that it should not be difficult to relax and enjoy social occasions. Just remember to shake hands.

"Setting a good table" is important to personal pride but is also a sign of hospitality. An invitation for *Abendbrot* (literally "evening bread") indicates the meal will be an informal one while *Abendessen* (evening meal) indicates a more formal dinner.

Thank-you notes, preferably handwritten, are expected after any kind of dinner or party in someone's home—unless you know your host and hostess extremely well.

**Toasts.** It is not good manners to drink at a party before the host. He will raise his wine glass to the lady on his right, then toast the health of the group. You should do the same when you are host. The most usual phrase is *zum Wohl* (to your health), but the host or hostess usually adds a few words of greeting or good wishes.

After this initial courtesy, people drink as they wish. Often there are toasts among guests initiated by the person of higher rank, with the lower-ranking guest returning the toast a little later in the evening. At the time, the toast is acknowledged with a smile and a little nod of the head. Between men and women, it is always the man who makes the overture first.

The clinking of glasses usually occurs only at some special event like New Year's or a birthday, and only glasses with wine or champagne are clinked together—never beer, brandy, or hard liquor. Hold a wine glass by its stem. Except when you are drinking brandy, it is considered bad form to hold a glass by its body, for this heats the wine too much.

**Informal Visits**. Germans are not accustomed to "dropping in" on one another. Among close friends and relatives, informal visits may occur during the Sunday coffee hour, but acquaintances and newcomers should phone before visiting. Phone calls during mealtime (between one and three o'clock and between six and eight) should be avoided. When possible, Germans prefer to eat their heavy meal in the middle of the day, but this is becoming increasingly difficult to accomplish because of modern work schedules and traffic.

Germans are generally rather reserved and prefer to allow others, especially foreigners, to make the first move. Inviting neighbors for coffee and dessert (or perhaps a glass of wine) on a weekend afternoon may lead to friendly relations, but you will probably have to take the initiative. The *Kaffeeklatsch* usually takes place in the afternoon—often the only time women can gather with their friends for "a coffee" at the café.

## CONVERSATION AND PERSONAL STYLE

It is easy to be poised when being introduced; all you need to do is shake hands and say *Guten Tag* (or *Guten Morgen* or *Guten Abend*), Frau (Herr).... You don't have to go on with *Wie geht es Ihnen* (How are you?) or any other phrase. *Wie geht es Ihnen* is intended as an inquiry about the well-being of someone you already know, and the answer may be quite detailed. (In fact, its use with a stranger or new acquaintance should be avoided; it is taken literally and therefore is quite personal and may offend.)

The best opening into anyone's language is genuine appreciation for the things of which the speakers of that language are proud. Too often we are not aware of these in another country and end up talking about ourselves. Try to open most conversations, particularly when you first arrive, with some complimentary and interested comment about the country, the city, sports, music, or whatever—not with a personal remark or question. Germans have a tremendous and justifiable pride in their extraordinary postwar economic growth, their historic towns and ancient architecture, and their famous musicians and artists. Spend some time learning about Germany's heroes, sources of pride, and accomplishments so that you can talk about them easily. You will find this contributes considerably to your conversation skills, for your companion will almost surely expand on any subject you mention with pleasure and you will be off to a good start.

Germans are private people and resent being asked personal questions by people they have just met. Many of the questions which Germans may consider too personal are the very ones considered appropriate by Americans as ice breakers—questions about occupation or spouse and family. Also to be avoided are questions concerning finances, educational background, religious affiliation, and the Holocaust. World War II can be discussed in the context of personal experiences. This situation changes when you get to know someone well, of course. Let your German friend take the lead in discussing sensitive topics.

When you get to know Germans well, you will find that they tend to be direct, even blunt, in conversation, unlike Americans, who, though they admire honesty, consider it more tactful to leave some things unsaid. The ability to impart knowledge is, to the German, an important skill to which politeness may occasionally take a back seat.

The German does not consider it impolite to comment on unusual dress or to point out misbehavior. Because they are concerned with honesty, they don't compliment often. A compliment is given only when a person has done something outstandingly well. If you give compliments too frequently, the German will be embarrassed or question your sincerity.

## NIGHT LIFE

Germans enjoy a lively night life, which often includes dancing. It is customary for women to dance with any male who asks them. Brush up on your waltzes and polkas. Although young people follow the latest dance fads and rock groups, the older generation keeps much to the more traditional styles of dancing.

Small neighborhood restaurants (similar to British pubs) abound and are called *Kniepen*. Many a pleasant evening can be spent in them eating, drinking, and just getting together.

If you go to a restaurant and find it crowded, don't be surprised if you are seated with strangers. The practice of sharing a table is quite common. It is sometimes difficult to get a glass of water in a restaurant. Germans, like most Europeans, are not accustomed to drinking water, and your waiter may ask you if you would like mineral water instead. Milk is also not commonly served; if you request it, you run the risk of being served warm milk.

## SUMMARY

Traditions are very important to Germans because they are manifestations of their culture and thus give a sense of security. Americans are much more willing to accept change since they are not bound by traditions, which they view as sentimental. They accept a trial-and-error approach to new ideas, whereas the Germans want to investigate to see if the new is better than the old before changing.

The following list summarizes some of the points discussed in this or other chapters and suggests appropriate behavior to use while you are learning more about German culture and behavior. Gaining an understanding of the cultural assumptions and values that are fundamental to German patterns of behavior is very important. The best way to learn is to observe and to ask for information when you do not understand or when you feel you may have done or said something inappropriate.

1.  Shake hands the first time you see a coworker or acquaintance that day (except on the street, unless you want to stop and talk), both on meeting and on bidding farewell.

2.  Teach your children to be polite when meeting Germans. They should shake hands and use a polite greeting, for example, "*Guten Tag, Herr Schmidt.*" At the beginning, a polite "how do you do" or "good morning" (afternoon, evening) is acceptable.

3.  Use a person's title when addressing him or her: *Herr/ Frau/Doktor....* If the person has more than one title, use the higher-ranking one, so you would address *Professor Doktor Mueller* as *Professor Mueller* (even though you may hear others using multiple honorifics).

4.  If you don't know a person's name, you may address him or her by title only (*Doktor, Professor, Direktor*).

5.  Don't address a German woman with her husband's first name (e.g., *Frau Hans Schmidt*); it is not customary.

6.  Address all adult men with *Herr* and adult women with *Frau*, whether they are married or not.

7.  Only use first names and *Du* when you have become very good friends. Let your German acquaintance take the lead in making the switch.

8.  Friendship involves considerable commitment and attention but is very rewarding. Don't be discouraged if it takes awhile.

9.  Always be polite and use good manners; a bad first impression is difficult to change.

10. Take flowers for your hostess when you are invited to someone's house.

11. Use your knife and fork European style, that is, keep the knife in your right hand, your fork in your left, and use the knife to push food onto the fork. If you are not using a knife, keep your right hand on the table next to the plate, not in your lap.

12. Do not drink until your host has drunk at the table. The proper toast is *Zum Wohl!* or *Prosit!* Glasses are clinked on special occasions and only when drinking wine or champagne.

13. Expect to be served coffee only after a meal (German coffee is normally stronger than American).

14. Remember to write a thank-you note after a dinner or party in someone's home.

15. Be prepared for a surprised look if you order milk or water in a restaurant; they are not commonly served.

16. Don't be surprised if strangers ask to sit down at your table in a restaurant, especially if the restaurant is crowded; this is quite customary. You are not expected to converse with the other people beyond *Guten Tag* and *Auf Wiedersehen.*

17. At New Year's, tip people who have been of service during the year, for example, the mailman, newspaper boy, cleaning lady, etc.

18. When staying in a hotel, tip the concierge if he or she has helped you with some special service. Usually the

concierge is the best source of information on sight-seeing, transportation, or theater tickets.

19. Don't rush a German. Remember, a job done well is more important than a job done quickly.

20. Be patient with red tape—there is a lot of it. Germany is a very regulated society.

21. Learn the language and have patience.

In general, don't expect Germans to be the same as Americans—they are products of different cultures and traditions.

# 5

# Doing Business in Germany

## LANGUAGE

Although a working knowledge of English is increasingly common among younger people, only an estimated 20 percent of older Germans speak English. If you use German, people will appreciate your effort, no matter how minimal your language skill or how imperfect your accent or pronunciation. Anything written in English should be accompanied by a German translation when presented in meetings or negotiations. Plan on taking an interpreter with you to any important conference. The burden is on you, the foreigner, to make sure you can communicate in an understandable manner. Translation services are readily available in the major cities, and major banks, trade fair administrations, or conference and convention centers can generally provide an interpreter. Another source of information and service is the Association of Translators and Interpreters: BOU (*Bundesverband der Dolmetscher und Ubersetzer* e.V.), 4100 Duisburg, Mulheimerstrasse; Tel: 357-480. Interpreters should be briefed before a meeting, especially if discussions are to be technical. In this case the interpreter should be provided, in advance, with a list of terms or technical words in order to become familiar with them before being required to translate them.

If you have drawings or specifications, they should be in German and in metrics. This preparation not only saves time but gives a far better impression. Be generous with business cards, advertising materials (in German), and samples. These all help to increase your chances of being directed to the correct department and seeing the most appropriate person.

## STYLE

Get to the point politely but quickly and know your subject well. The Germans are a thorough people who do not like their time wasted. The sort of preliminary courtesies and flourishes that are required among Spanish, French, or Italians are wasted on Germans. After greetings and introductions (and a few brief comments on the weather or the most recent soccer match), they are anxious to get on with the job at hand; they do not like to chat before doing business. Formality is important as well, so avoid a breezy approach. Many people you meet will seem quite reserved, and it may take time to develop personal contacts, especially among those who have had little previous experience with foreign firms. (The younger your counterparts are, the friendlier and more informal they will be, as is true in other situations.) But, reserved or not, most businesspeople will offer liquid refreshment to office visitors (coffee, alcoholic beverages, or both). You should be prepared to do the same in your office.

Germans are working hard to hold their own domestic markets, which are under heavy competition from Japan and other Common Market countries. They give close and critical scrutiny to all new ideas and will look hard at both quality and price. Be prepared; make concrete, precise offers; confirm all agreements in writing. Approaches should be carefully planned. "Playing it by ear" is not appreciated and won't get you far. Breaking an appointment or arriving even a few minutes late is a quick way to give a bad impression. A German may be so insulted by your poor manners that he or she will fail to hear your proposal, no matter how good it is. Germans are tough, good negotiators; they have a reputation for keeping their bargains, and they expect others to do the same.

Northern Germans are more reserved and efficient than southern Germans, whose lifestyle is much more relaxed. Whether you are in the north or the south, however, start all first meetings with considerable formality and continue in this manner until your German host or counterpart suggests otherwise. Use titles and last names when addressing your colleagues, and be particularly careful to avoid addressing secretaries by their first names. One needs to remember to shake hands on all occasions and to show respect for those of greater age or rank by such small courtesies as opening doors, helping with coats, or standing when they enter a room. Keep your jacket on and your tie pulled tight; avoid putting your feet on desks, chairs, or train seats; sit up at your desk instead of leaning back with your hands behind your head. These are small things, but they give an impression of sloppiness in a country where proper behavior is important.

You will find that most northern Europeans, and definitely the British and Germans, value privacy and tend to close their office doors. This reflects a deep psychological difference from most Americans, who feel an open door is friendly and a closed one is aloof. The closed door is a manifestation of the German's need for order and privacy, rather than an indication of aloofness. It also helps to keep the office or room warm, and in a country where heating costs are high, this is important. There is yet another reason for the closed door: it serves as an indicator to employees that they can work without the boss leaning over their shoulders.

It is hard to meet the top people in big German corporations and impossible without an appointment made well ahead of time. German directors delegate a great deal to lesser executives, and do little that does not directly concern their own job assignments.

Managers who sign *p.p.a.* before their names have the authority to negotiate for the organization's management. This stands for *Prokurist*, meaning "manager with registered signing authority." An executive who signs *i.v.* with his or her name has the power to negotiate in some special areas for the firm. It means *in Vollmacht*, "with authority."

An important point to remember is that under both German and Swiss law, if you induce a party to believe a contract will be concluded and the contract does not materialize, you may be liable for damages. Be careful in this area, especially if your command of German is shaky.

## BUSINESS ENTERTAINING

If you are invited to a restaurant, do not try to pay the bill. In general, the person who does the inviting for a business lunch or dinner picks up the tab. Luncheon engagements should be made for around 1300 (most do not like to eat earlier) and supper appointments for about 1830. Business luncheons usually last about an hour or an hour and a half. Dinner invitations are normally for 2000 and generally include spouses. Since German businesspeople try to keep private and business relations separate, an invitation to a home is quite an honor. Read the section, "Social Customs," in chapter 4 for dining etiquette.

It is not considered appropriate to discuss business outside the office. A business lunch may include some business talk, but even then the conversation will tend to be more general. Outside office hours—over golf or dinner, for example—avoid discussing business entirely.

## SERVICES AVAILABLE TO U.S. BUSINESSES IN GERMANY

The U.S. Commerce Department's Product Marketing Service provides a base of operation in key areas for the use of American exporters while they are conducting business overseas.

This service is especially helpful in aiding you before and during participation in trade fairs. Germany has many fairs throughout the year and the Commerce Department can provide information on setting up displays and on obtaining space and publicity. For a daily fee, American businesspeople may rent space for up to five days in U.S. Trade Centers in London, Paris, Frankfurt, Milan, and Stockholm as well as in other places around the world.

Services include telephones, audiovisual equipment, secretarial and interpreting assistance, and a list of key business prospects.

For further information, contact the U.S. Department of Commerce in your area or the Export Development Office, International Trade Administration, U.S. Department of Commerce, Washington, DC 20230.

## HIERARCHY IN GERMAN COMPANIES

Both the German and American systems are outlined, but it is important to remember that a direct comparison between the two is not possible.

### The German System

*Aktiengesellschaft* (AG) employing more than five hundred people:

1. *Aufsichtsrat*—nonexecutive supervisory or advisory board elected by (a) the shareholders or their representatives and (b) the employees (codetermination) (Unlike the U.S. practice, members of the board of management may not be members of the supervisory board. The supervisory board appoints and supervises the *Vorstand*.)

2. *Vorstand*—board of management, or executive board
   *Vorsitzer* (also *Vorsitzender*)—chairman, president
   *Stellvertretender Vorsitz des Vorstandes*—deputy chairman of the board
   *Ordentliches Mitglied des Vorstandes*—regular member of the board
   *Stellvertretendes Mitglied des Vorstandes*—deputy member of the board

3. *Generalbevollmächtigter*—general manager
*Abteilungsleiter*—division/department head
*Prokurist*—corporate secretary

## American System

Joint Stock Corporation:

1. Board of Directors—includes the president and possibly several executive vice presidents of the corporation

2. Management Group—includes the president, the senior vice president, and the executive vice president

3. General Manager—includes the assistant general manager and departmental managers

## SUMMARY SUGGESTIONS

The following suggestions summarize German business customs. It is important to become familiar with business practices in Germany, and some resources to help you are listed in the bibliography.

1. Always be on time for appointments; even a few minutes make a difference.

2. Be direct in all your business dealings; get to the point quickly and stay there.

3. Use direct eye contact and a formal approach; avoid breezy sales pitches.

4. Your body language should also reflect formality (no loose ties, shoes on desks, slouched posture).

5. Never sell a method or product on the merit that it is American—what works for Americans does not necessarily work for Germans.

6. Don't assume your coworkers can speak English.

7. Anything written in English should be translated into German for meetings.

8. Find your own interpreter; don't expect your German counterpart to find one for you.

9. Convert relevant measurements to metric before making a presentation or submitting a report.

10. Remember to shake hands with all your associates the first time you see them each day and again upon departure in the evening.

11. Always call all your employees, including secretaries, by their title and last names; it is a sign of respect.

12. Offer liquid refreshment (coffee or alcoholic beverages) to office guests.

13. The person who does the inviting for a business lunch pays the bill. Although gratuity is included, special service warrants an additional tip.

14. Do not mix business with social occasions. Even business lunches tend to be social in nature.

15. Make concrete offers and be definite; your proposal will be carefully scrutinized.

# 6

# Household Pointers

## HOUSING

Although housing is in short supply all over Europe, the situation is critical in Germany. Modern, well-designed satellite towns have been and are being built near many of the cities, partly to supply new housing and partly to eliminate city slums. Unfortunately, this construction has supplied nowhere near the amount of housing needed.

Your housing search is likely to be slow and tedious, so be prepared for a lengthy stay at a hotel. In addition to hotels, be sure to inquire about pensions; "holiday villages" are another possibility, especially if you have children (inquire at the local tourist office). Whatever your temporary quarters, you will want to be sure to carry (not ship) books, children's games, hobbies, language materials, and whatever else you think you will need during the first few weeks.

When you are looking for housing, keep in mind that location is more important than the number of rooms you have or the size of refrigerator that will fit. Experienced sojourners in Germany recommend that you conduct your house hunting with one eye on the subway, bus, or tram system. If you have children, being located near the school, or in an area with access to transportation to the school, will be especially helpful.

There are several ways of going about your housing search. Real estate agencies are one option. Although German real estate agents are available, you may be able to find British or American real estate agencies through the chamber of commerce, your consulate, or bank. Many English-speaking expatriates have found these to be more helpful. Another possibility is the housing bureau (*Wohnungsamt*) of your city, which usually maintains a list of apartments. The Municipal Tourist Office (*Verkehrsamt*), a kind of cross between a chamber of commerce and tourist bureau, can provide you with a list of apartments, houses, or pensions where you can stay while searching for permanent housing and can sometimes provide long-term housing information.

## Renting

Rent control ended in 1969; consequently, rents are high, and the real estate agent's fee may be as much as two months' rent. Rents are based on square meters and, in general, are comparable to those in New York City.

When reading newspaper ads, there are several important words to watch for.

*Leere Wohnung* (unfurnished apartment) means exactly what it says, often down to even the towel racks, light fixtures, and mirrors. Built-in closets are rare, more often wardrobes (armoires) are used and are supplied by the tenant.

*Möblierte Wohnung* (furnished apartment).

*Möblierte Zimmer* (furnished room).

*Komfort* indicates medium price, central heat, and good plumbing.

*Luxus* indicates quality decor and fittings, more luxury.

*Einfach* means "plain" and could even indicate that the kitchen and bath are shared.

*Kaltmiete* means that the heat is not included in the rent.

Some other terms and abbreviations you may see in the real estate listing include the following:

| | |
|---|---|
| NB | *Neubau* (new construction) |
| *Erstbezug* | First occupancy |
| *Provision* | Agent's fee, usually two months' rent |
| *NK* | *Nebenkosten* (utilities) |
| *Kaution* | Deposit against damage |
| *Auflösung* | Take-over fee, usually asked by previous tenant for furnishings |
| *VB* | *Vereinbarung* (price negotiable) |
| *DHH* | *Doppelhaushalt* (duplex) |
| *REH* or *RHM* | Row house, corner; row house, middle |

**Leases**. Normally leases are written for two years, with a three-month notice for either party. The landlord cannot put you out without cause and even with cause must go to court to do so.

Be sure that you understand every word in the lease. A common clause, *Schönheitsreparaturen*, translates as "beauty repairs" but really implies that the tenant must completely renovate the property when leaving. This used to be taken for granted but is no longer justified, given the high rents and short-term leases.

At the time you sign the lease, you will be asked to pay a three-month advance called "caution money." Like a security deposit, this money is kept as a guarantee that the tenant will pay for all necessary repairs accrued during tenancy. You should make sure that money is deposited in an interest-bearing account for you, not the landlord. In addition, to protect yourself from having to pay repairs for problems that existed before you moved in, make a careful inventory of all cracks, signs of wear in plumbing, peeling paint, holes, etc., and have your landlord initial the inventory before you sign the lease. Otherwise, most or all of your caution money will be eaten up with costly repairs instead of being returned to you. In short, be extremely thorough in protecting yourself. If you leave before the lease expires, you must sublet the apartment or house, forfeit the caution money, or pay the rent until the landlord finds a new tenant.

In many parts of Germany you, the occupant, are responsible for assisting in the maintenance of the yard, basement, halls, and sidewalks of an apartment house. You may also be responsible for repairs that are necessary while you live in the rented house or apartment. The law requires that the occupant of a house with a chimney hire a chimney sweep to clean the chimney every two or three months.

**House Rules (*Hausordnungen*).** Be sure to inquire about the house rules, regulations which apply to both apartments and houses and which are generally unfamiliar to Americans. Some common rules include the following: (1) no baths late or early, (2) restrictions on when and how loudly you can play your radio/stereo/TV, (3) requirements such as locking an outside door after 2000 (difficult when you give a party). Ask about the hours and extent to which children may play in the garden, etc. It should now be fairly obvious that renting is an ordeal—expensive and fraught with risk and unexpected expenses. The best advice is to proceed with caution and find someone knowledgeable and experienced to help you.

## Home Purchase

Although housing costs are high and real estate agents' commissions may be as much as 5 percent of the purchase price, you may decide it is financially advisable to purchase a home or apartment, even for a two- or three-year stay. If so, make arrangements directly with a savings or loan company yourself; don't negotiate the financing through the real estate agent. This can save you the 5 percent fee the agent receives for arranging financing. (This is in addition to the sales commission.) About one-third of the purchase price is usually required as a down payment; loan rates vary as in the U.S.

New construction is exempt from property taxes, but you can expect to pay high installation costs for electricity, water pipes, and the like, as well as yearly fees in proportion to your frontage for such things as sewer maintenance. If you buy an apartment (quite expensive), your maintenance charges will be relatively low.

## ELECTRICITY AND APPLIANCES

German current runs on 220 volts-50 cycles, which means that if you are coming from a country using 110 volts-60 cycles, you will need to think carefully about what appliances to bring with you and what to buy locally.

Foreign nationals throughout Europe recommend that you leave as much electrical equipment behind as you can and buy locally. Since Germany is particularly well known for the quality of its electrical appliances, finding what you want should present no problems. German prices vary from reasonable to expensive, but you can be assured the appliance is built to last. Whatever you buy can be resold before your return home. In fact, a good source of 220 volt-50 cycle appliances is a family returning home.

What you decide to bring and to leave at home will, of course, depend on your family's needs, the age of your equipment, length of stay, and so on, but the following are some general guidelines to help you with your decision.

All 110-volt appliances can be used with a transformer; however, those that must operate at a specific speed (clocks, record players, tape recorders, etc.) will have to be adapted to 50 cycles. These are probably best left at home. Television sets are another good candidate for storage at home since European television operates on a different standard. American TVs can, however, be used for Nintendo and other video games, and for watching American video tapes. If you bring American videotapes, you must also bring an American standard video playback machine. Because a good battery-powered radio is essential, we suggest that you ship your own or plan on buying one (preferably a high-quality shortwave radio) on arrival.

German refrigerators are small, stoves tend to heat slowly, and clothes driers are rare, so you may wish to bring these appliances with you. Since German washing machines heat their own water (only cold water is piped in), it is a good idea to purchase a washing machine locally.

While making decisions about appliances, you may want to consider the following points. German (and European in general) rooms are small, and there is often not enough space for full-size U.S. appliances. Many houses are not wired to carry a heavy load, and electricity is expensive; you can, however, have the local electricity board—which also sells appliances—check your wiring at no cost. And finally, your warranties may not be effective outside the country of purchase. If you do decide to bring your own appliances, be sure to bring spare parts and instruction manuals with you, and bear in mind that you will probably encounter difficulties with repair. Most major cities in the U.S. have at least one store that sells appliances made specifically for export (220 volt-50 cycle). Small appliances with universal motors that operate on either 110/60 or 220/50 are available.

Plug adapters are necessary because German outlets require round, pronged plugs that are deep enough to make connection. Local hardware stores and stores that sell appliances for export are good sources for plug adapters and transformers (necessary if you plan to use U.S. 110 volt-60 cycle appliances).

Obtaining a telephone in Germany can be quite an ordeal due to the shortage of phone lines, so try to rent a house or apartment with one already installed. Phones are rented, not purchased, and you are charged for installation and billed monthly for your calls. If you cannot take over a phone from the previous tenant, you may have to wait for as long as a year to obtain one. Foreigners are assessed a deposit of about DM 100 upon installation. This deposit can be deducted from your phone bill after six months; don't forget to do so. Basic phone service charges run about U.S. $25-$30 per month (subject to change of course).

## HOUSEHOLD HELP

Most expatriates have household help—generally a cleaning woman who comes on a weekly basis. The best way to find help is through neighbors or with their help. Try *Amerika Haus* (German-American clubs described in chapter 10) contacts or talk with other expatriates, who may recommend their employee to you; or ask the owners of the small neighborhood stores if they know of available help. Sometimes wives of EEC workers from other countries are looking for domestic work. Local clergy can sometimes be helpful since they know the local residents.

Baby-sitters are also found by word-of-mouth, through neighbors or through nearby schools and universities. In addition, Europe has a highly developed *au pair* system. An au pair is a live-in student who wishes to perfect his or her English. An au pair essentially becomes a member of the family, baby-sitting at night and studying during the day. If you are interested in this kind of arrangement, ask at the local bureau of employment or at the nearest univerity. Another source of baby-sitters is the local newspaper. Check the ads or place your own.

Unless you plan on having live-in help from the U.S. or another country outside the EEC, you will not need visas or permits for your help. You should, however, check with the local tax board or commune office to determine wage rates, taxes, and social security payments that must be paid.

## SHOPPING

Supermarkets and department stores are on the increase, but most Germans still do most of their shopping at small specialized stores. You should try to follow their lead. It is an easy way to meet your neighbors and establish relationships with local store-keepers. You can also practice your German so long as you don't try to shop at peak hours when shopkeepers can't spend much time with you. Some of the most common specialty shops follow:

| | |
|---|---|
| *Bäckerei* | bakery |
| *Metzgerei, Fleischerei* | butcher shop |
| *Lebensmittelgeschäft* | grocery store |
| *Wein und Spirituosen* | liquor store |
| *Feinkost* | delicatessen |
| *Buchhandlung* | bookstore |
| *Obst- und Gemüseladen* | fruit and vegetable store |
| *Kaufhaus, Warenhaus* | department store |
| *Herrenbekleidungsgeschäft* | men's clothing store |
| *Damenbekleidungsgeschäft* | women's clothing store |
| *Spielwaren* | toy store |
| *Tabakwarenladen* | tobacco store |

Weekly markets, where farmers sell their own produce, are the best—and least expensive—source of fresh produce, jams, pickles, plants, etc. (Health regulations prohibit the touching of fruits and vegetables before they are purchased.)

Buying meat can be a bewildering and often frustrating experience. The following German translations for cuts of meat may be helpful.

### *Rindfleisch*—beef

*Hochrippe*—prime rib
*Filet, Roastbeef*—sirloin
*Lendenstück*—tenderloin
*Rumpsteak*—sirloin top
*Keule mit Hinterhesse*—round with rump and shank
*Rindskeule*—round of beef
*Schwanzstück*—rump
*Keule*—leg
*Lappen*—flank
*Bruststück*—brisket
*Rippenstücke*—ribs
*Beefsteak*—steak

## Schweinefleisch—pork

*Schulter*—shoulder of pork
*Vorderschinken*—shoulder of ham
*Kotelettstücke*—loin chops
*Lende*—loin
*Haxen*—hocks
*Schinken*—ham
*Schinkenspeck*—bacon
*Rippenspeere*—spare ribs

## Hammelfleisch—mutton

## Lammenfleisch—lamb

*Vorderkeule*—shoulder
*Koteletten*—chops
*Nierenstück*—roast loin
*Brust*—breast

*Geschäft, Handlung,* and *Laden* all mean "shop." One store which might cause you some confusion is the *Drogerie.* The German drugstore sells nonprescription drugs, cosmetics, and household goods but no magazines, candy, or cigarettes—and no prescription drugs. To buy prescription drugs, you go to an *Apotheke.* All the *Apotheken* in town take turns being open at night in case of emergency.

The hours and days that the shops are open vary and are often confusing. Some are permitted by law to be open on Sundays; for example, in most cities milk shops are open in the morning, flower shops around noon, and bakeries in the afternoon. Shops generally close at 1400 on Saturdays except for the first Saturday in the month when they remain open until 1800. This variation results from federal laws that were enacted to protect the interests of shop personnel (particularly small shopkeepers who cannot afford the extra staff required to stay open long hours) and to keep working hours within mandated weekly limits.

On entering small shops, you should greet shopkeepers with *Guten Tag* (or in Bavaria, *Grüss Gott*) and, when you leave, say *Auf Wiedersehen*. Don't be surprised if the shopkeeper walks you to the door and opens it for you as you leave. This is a polite gesture, not an attempt to rush you out. In small shops, you normally wait to be helped, but in large stores you may have to ask a salesperson to assist you.

Waiting in line is not the usual practice, so customers must be rather aggressive about protecting their turn. Because prices are fixed, bargaining is inappropriate. You are expected to carry a shopping bag in which to put your parcels. These are generally small, expandable, and made of string or plastic. If you have forgotten your bag, some will be available for purchase. Browsing in stores is not a common practice; one usually makes the purchase and leaves.

Sales are held twice a year (the end of January and July) and extend over a two-week period. These are end-of-season sales, and prices are reduced substantially. You can find goods at reduced prices during the rest of the year in most shops, marked as *Sonderangebot*. There are also weekly throwaway newspapers which advertise all the local bargains.

If possible, avoid shopping during lunch hour, between 1700 and 1800, and on Saturdays because the stores are most crowded then. In general, you will find the staff in most stores helpful and polite.

Be prepared to watch your diet. Germany is the land of dumplings and strudel, pastries, sausages, cheeses, and beer. Although you can get frozen or canned foods from abroad, they are very expensive. The quicker you can shift to the wide variety of local brands, the better. The Germans love to eat, and German food is delicious.

## Beverages

You will be able to find whatever you like to drink in Germany. Water is safe almost everywhere and milk is pasteurized, but most

Germans prefer to drink wine, beer, or bottled mineral water with their meals. Alcoholic drinks such as scotch, bourbon, and martinis are available but are much more expensive than beer or wine.

If wine is your specialty, you will want to become knowledgeable about German wines. Mastering a few fundamentals about the wine regions by which wines are distinguished and classified is the best way to begin; next learn the vineyards and, finally, the vintage years. Many pamphlets and books are available on the subject. Picking the right wine is a real art and a source of great pleasure.

If you are a beer lover, you are probably already familiar with at least a few German beers and you can have a marvelous time trying out the whole gamut—from light beers to the many heavy and dark varieties. The strongest are called "exports." During the business day, you may want to drink *Ausschank*, an excellent, light tap beer. Among the pilsner beers, the best are still from Czechoslovakia although German pilsners have improved considerably. Ask German acquaintances to recommend brands of beer. They love to do so and will often start animated conversations as they discuss the varieties among themselves and tell you the differences.

In German restaurants, beer is served in one-half liter glasses (except in Bavaria). In Munich you may find yourself drinking from liter mugs (just under a quart) called *Masskruge.*

# Measurements

Unless you intend to carry a calculator around with you when you go shopping, you will find dealing with weights and measurements much easier if you think metrically.

| | |
|---|---|
| 1 gram (g) | 0.035 ounce |
| 1 kilogram--for short, kilo (1,000 gram) | 2.2 pounds |
| 1 centimeter (cm) | 0.3937 inch |
| 2.54 centimeters | 1 inch |
| 1 meter (m) | 3.280 feet |
| 1,609.3 meters | 1 mile |
| 1 kilometer | 0.625 mile |

### Liquid Measure

| | |
|---|---|
| 1 liter (l) | 2.113 pints |
| 1 liter | 1.056 quarts |
| 3.785 liters | 1 gallon |

### Dry measure

| | |
|---|---|
| 1 liter | 0.908 quart |
| 1 decaliter (10 liters) | 1.135 pecks |
| 1 hectoliter (100 liters) | 2.837 bushels |

### For conversion of recipes:

| | |
|---|---|
| 1 cup of sugar | 200 grams |
| 1 cup of flour | 150 grams |
| 1 teaspoon | 5 grams |
| 1 tablespoon | 12 grams |
| 1 pound | 450 grams |
| 1 kilo | 2.2 pounds |

# For conversion of Fahrenheit into Centigrade (Celsius)

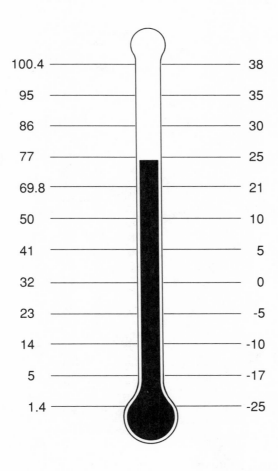

| Fahrenheit | Centigrade |
|---|---|
| 100.4 | 38 |
| 95 | 35 |
| 86 | 30 |
| 77 | 25 |
| 69.8 | 21 |
| 50 | 10 |
| 41 | 5 |
| 32 | 0 |
| 23 | -5 |
| 14 | -10 |
| 5 | -17 |
| 1.4 | -25 |

# Clothing

Clothing sizes used in both the U.S. and Europe are noted on the chart below. Once you have identified your size, there should be no problem in finding clothes that fit. Children's sizes generally go by age and/or weight.

## Skirts, Dresses, Coats

| U.S. | Europe |
|------|--------|
| 10 | 38 |
| 12 | 40 |
| 14 | 42 |
| 16 | 44 |
| 18 | 46 |
| 20 | 48 |

## Shoes

| U.S. | Europe |
|------|--------|
| 6 | 37 |
| 7 | 38 |
| 8 | 39 |
| 9 | 40 |
| 10 | 41 |
| 11 | 42 |
| 12 | 43 |
| 13 | 44 |

## Shirts

| U.S. | Europe |
|------|--------|
| 14 | 36 |
| 14 1/2 | 37 |
| 15 | 38 |
| 15 1/2 | 39 |
| 16 | 41 |
| 16 1/2 | 42 |
| 17 | 43 |

## Suits

| U.S. | Europe |
|------|--------|
| 36 | 46 |
| 38 | 48 |
| 40 | 50 |
| 42 | 52 |
| 44 | 54 |
| 46 | 56 |
| 48 | 58 |

## Hats

| U.S. | Europe |
|------|--------|
| 30 | 38 |
| 32 | 40 |
| 34 | 42 |
| 36 | 44 |
| 38 | 46 |
| 40 | 48 |

## Hats

| U.S. | Europe |
|------|--------|
| 7 | 57 |
| 7 1/8 | 58 |
| 7 1/4 | 59 |
| 7 3/8 | 60 |
| 7 1/2 | 61 |

Here are some tips for easy conversion of U.S. clothing sizes to German sizes:

For blouses, add 8 to your U.S. size to get the German size; for example, if you wear a 34 U.S. you'll take a 42 German. For dresses and skirts, you'll have to add 28 to your U.S. size. For shoes, you add 31. For example, size 6 would become size 37.

# 7

# Health and Medical Care

Because most of Germany has a moderate climate without extremes in temperature, you will probably not encounter many health problems, except for respiratory difficulties—colds, bronchitis, and similar ailments—or rheumatic conditions which are aggravated by the dampness. The quality and purity of the drinking water, dairy products, and other foods are strictly controlled by government inspectors. The standards for community sanitation and cleanliness are extremely high.

If you do become ill, you will be in good hands. German health standards are excellent, and the standards in the field of medicine and medical practice are exemplified by their excellent hospitals. They are world leaders in the fields of pharmaceuticals, optics, and hearing aids.

Doctors' office hours are normally between 1000-1200 and 1600-1700 (except Wednesdays and weekends). Each doctor posts his or her hours in a readily visible place outside the office.

Germany has a competent emergency service. Anyone in need may call *Aertlich Notdienst*, listed in the local telephone directory, for information on and phone numbers for those doctors on call.

The following organizations provide information, by location, on English-speaking doctors worldwide.

1.   **IAMAT** (International Association for Medical Assistance

to Travelers): in the U.S., 736 Center Street, Lewiston, New York 14092.

This organization is highly recommended for and by travelers. For a donation you will receive a packet of information including a list of medical centers affiliated with IAMAT and staffed by English-speaking doctors. There are IAMAT centers in most major cities throughout Germany.

2. **INTERMEDIC:** 777 Third Avenue, New York, New York 10017.

Membership in INTERMEDIC can be obtained for a small fee. This organization supplies a membership card and a list of English-speaking physicians in two hundred cities around the world who have agreed to a set fee schedule.

## Health Insurance Plan

Medical costs have risen more sharply in Germany than in other parts of Europe. You may want to look into acquiring state insurance coverage (*Krankenkasse*) if your salary is paid in DMs. Eighty-eight percent of the population is covered by the plan and report that its services are excellent. Foreign nationals living in Germany are eligible for the benefits of this health insurance plan.

All care is free to insured persons, up to a maximum of about U.S. $1,200. This includes professional consultations and medical examinations, surgery, therapy, convalescent care, home nursing, psychotherapy, pharmaceuticals, and dental care (both mainte-nance and prosthetics) as well as a generous death payment. This is one of the most comprehensive insurance systems in the world. It is under the general supervision of the Federal Ministry of Labor and Social Affairs and is administered through local insurance offices.

The employer and employee each pay half of the insurance payments. Those insured may select their physicians from the membership (most of Germany's doctors and dentists are members of the plan) and may change doctors at any time. They may also choose their hospital, if authorized by the physician, and will have semiprivate accommodations unless the illness requires a private room. (Anyone can pay the difference and have a private room.) During a hospitalization period, the health insurance plan provides a maintenance allowance to meet current expenses. If you are insured in the U.S. by your employer, this insurance may cover your international needs as well. If it does, pay medical bills and submit them along with a description of the treatment for reimbursement.

## Spas

There are more than 250 registered spas, featuring not only modern therapeutic care of all sorts (thermal, mineral, etc.) but also providing entertainment and sports to speed the recuperative process. The cost of three or four vacation days, including treatment, is low.

You can get a list of all-inclusive spa vacations from either of the following: Deutsches Reisebüro GmbH, D 6 Frankfurt/Main, Eschersheimer Landstrasse 25/27 or Deutscher Baederverband, D 53 Bonn, Schumannstrasse 111.

# 8

# Schools

## INTERNATIONAL OR LOCAL: IT'S YOUR CHOICE

For many children, attending school in another culture is a tremendously valuable experience. At the primary level, most children can adapt successfully to European schools without prior knowledge of the host-country language because the basic curricula are similar and language learning comes more easily to young children. However, European curricula, educational systems, and educational philosophies vary greatly at the middle school, junior and senior high school, and university levels.

Each alternative has positive and negative aspects. When you and your child(ren) are thinking about local or American/international schools, consider all the possibilities before making a final decision. School choice is one of the most important decisions you will need to make while you are abroad. This international experience (centered, for your child, in and around his or her prime activity—school) will help set the tone for your child's future.

Prior to making your decision, visit the available schools. With your child(ren), make a list of all the questions and concerns you have regarding each school and its programs. Try not to judge a school by its lavish or spartan appearance. A school should be considered in the light of many criteria: fulfillment of your child's needs and, of course, personal preference, not to mention affordability.

In choosing a school at any level, you need to consider your child's goals and interests. If your child is especially interested in sports or other extracurricular activities, the international or American school will probably be a better match than the local school. Most local education outside of the U.S. focuses on academics even in the lower grades. If your child learns quickly, is a strong student, and enjoys new challenges, a local school may be a wise choice, allowing for the opportunity to learn and use a second language and a new culture.

If you will be returning to your own country before your children complete high school or its equivalent, another consideration is acceptability and transferability of credits. Because of the differences in curricula, teaching methods, and diploma requirements, transferring between national systems is difficult and may result in loss of credit for course work completed. Math is a good example of these differences: in a U.S. high school, a student takes algebra I followed by geometry and trigonometry. In some European systems these courses are taught simultaneously over a period of three or four years. This is also true for the sciences. Finding a school offering a compatible curriculum, transferable credits, and similar completion requirements can eliminate at least one of the problems your child(ren) may face on returning home.

The following list of questions may help you in making your decision about a local or American/international school.

## Primary Level (fourth grade and below)

**Environment**: Is the general atmosphere warm and relaxed or conservative and strict? Do the students seem happy, well adjusted?

**Facilities**: Is there a library? If so, is it adequate? Is there a gym? Is there a nurse on staff, an infirmary?

**Curriculum/activities:** What is included in the curriculum at your child's grade level? How does this match what he or she has studied? Are music, art, and physical education a part of the curriculum? What other activities are available (Boy and Girl Scout programs, team sports, music lessons, etc.)?

**Parental involvement:** What is the level of parental involvement in classroom activities? Is there a PTA, a school board?

## Intermediate and Secondary Level

**Costs:** Is there tuition, and if so, what is it and what is included? What additional fees and charges can be expected (excursions, lab fees, etc.)?

**School population:** What percentage of the students are foreign, what local? What is the average class size? What is the ratio of staff to students?

**Academics:** What is the academic and national background of the teachers? Are remedial classes offered? Is tutorial help available? Do the majority of graduates go to a college or university, and if so, where? Are credits from the school readily accepted by high schools and/or universities in your home country?

**Counseling:** Is career and/or college guidance available, and if so, who is responsible for it? What other types of counseling and assistance are available?

**Activities:** What extracurricular activities are available? Are there required (optional) trips, and are there additional costs for trips and activities? Are art and music a part of the curriculum?

**Athletics:** Is physical education a part of the curriculum? What sports are available—team sports, extracurricular?

**Student responsibility:** Is cooperative work required/available (library, cafeteria, offices, etc.)? Is there a student government and if so, what is its role and responsibility?

**Discipline:** What are the school rules and how are infractions handled? What methods of discipline are used? Who is responsible for determining and carrying out disciplinary actions?

For a comparison between U.S. and European schools as well as information on accreditation of U.S. schools and the International Baccalaureate Diploma, see the appendix.

## GERMAN SCHOOLS

The German school system is excellent. As in the U.S., schools are under the control of the individual states, and curriculum and administrative policies and procedures vary, as do the costs. Public schools are government (state) supported, but fees are charged for some services and activities. School is mandatory only through ninth grade (or for nine years), and children can repeat every grade if necessary. German private schools are known for their high standards. Some offer classes in English, but most have long waiting lists for entry.

The educational program consists of an elementary stage and two secondary stages. Although most German children between the ages of three and six attend kindergarten, compulsory education begins at age six and continues until age fifteen. The primary stage includes kindergarten and four years of primary school. Primary schools provide the children with basic knowledge and skills in all the traditional academic subjects.

Class size is usually limited to between twenty and thirty pupils. Five or six class periods per day with different teachers for each subject are the rule. School is dismissed in the early afternoon, but children have a considerable amount of homework.

Secondary education (grade five and above) is closely linked to the trades, business, or professions that students plan to pursue and is intended to train students to fulfill the needs of society rather than to offer equal educational opportunities for all.

Educational and career decisions are made early, and work experience is considered an important part of the educational process. After the fourth grade, the first selective process divides children into three middle-level programs: *Hauptschule, Realschule,* and *Gymnasium* (some states have an orientation level—*Orientierungsstufe*—for fifth and sixth grades). Typically, Gymnasium leads to university, Realschule to specialized education or technical training, and Hauptschule to vocational training. Selection among the three options is based on the students' grades and aptitude and on parental preference. As shown in the diagram below, another decision must be made upon completion of ninth or tenth grade. At this point, the decision rests not only on performance in school and the interests of the student but on the students' financial resources and on competition through tests and academic achievement for a place in the school of choice. As the diagram suggests, it is possible to continue one's education through any route if the student is determined, is successful in gaining admission, and has the financial resources necessary.

**Structure of the Education System**

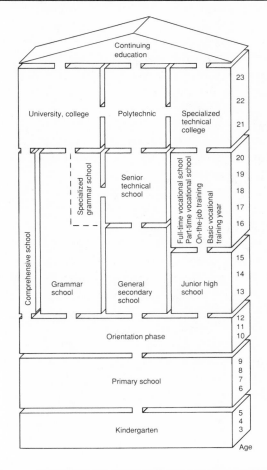

# ENGLISH LANGUAGE SCHOOLS

American, British, and international schools have been established in most of the major cities in Germany.

## American Schools

The following American schools are open to any child—American, host country, or international.

**John F. Kennedy Schule Berlin**, 1000 Berlin 37 (Zehlendorf), Teltower Damm 87-93.

Over thirteen hundred children in grades kindergarten through thirteen attend this school. Of these about six hundred are from the United States, six hundred from Germany, and about fifty from other nations. Nearly half of the one hundred faculty members are American, and the school follows an American curriculum.

**American International School of Düsseldorf**, 4000 Düsseldorf 31, Leuchtenberger Kirchweg 2 (or APO New York 09080).

This school includes prekindergarten through twelfth grade, with an enrollment of over three hundred, half of whom are in grades one through six. Of the total student population, about 170 are American, thirty are German, and one hundred are from other countries. Most of the faculty are American, as is the curriculum.

**The Frankfurt International School**, 6370 Oberursel/Taunus, An der Waldlust 5-7.

Classes for the nearly twelve hundred students range from kindergarten through thirteenth grade. Approximately half of the school's population is American; the remainder of the students are about evenly divided between Germans and other country nationals. Most of the full-time faculty are American, as is the curriculum.

**Internationale Schule Hamburg**, 2000 Hamburg 52, Holmbrook 20.

Kindergarten through grade twelve are offered in this school. Of the 550 students, approximately 250 are from the U.S.; the rest are from Germany and other countries. At least half of the faculty is American, as is the curriculum.

**Munich International School**, 8136 Percha über Starnberg, Schloss Buchhof.

With grades K-12 as well as a nursery school program, this school has an enrollment of over six hundred students, mostly American. It offers an American curriculum, supplemented with courses in German language and culture.

## Department of Defense Schools

The U.S. Department of Defense operates a number of elementary and secondary schools in Germany. These are identical in curriculum, activity offerings, and standards with U.S. public high schools. These are open on a space-available basis to nonmilitary American children. This option is not a dependable one, however, because these schools are required to provide education to all DOD dependents, and are, therefore, often filled to capacity and unavailable to private-sector dependents.

## International Schools

The following English-language schools offer either a German or International Baccalaureate Diploma curriculum.

**Euregio Gymnasium**, Akademie Klausenhof, 4236 Hamminkeln 2, Klausenhofstrasse 100.

**Europaische Schule Karlsruhe**, 7500 Karlsruhe-Waldtstadt, Albert-Schweitzer-Strasse 1.

**Europaische Schule München**, 8000 München 83, Elisa-Aulinger-Strasse 21.

## English-Language Preschools

**American Nursery Play School** (ages three to five)—Bonn.
**British Embassy Preparatory School** (grades 1-9)—Bonn.
**Children's Center** (ages thirty-three months to five)—Berlin.
**Carl Schurz School** (ages three to five)—Frankfurt.
**Kindergarten Erbe** (ages three to six)—Hamburg.

## UNIVERSITIES

Germany's thirty-one universities are lively centers of activity, as are its nine technical institutions and one hundred music, theological, and other postsecondary schools. If you can speak German, you may visit or audit courses at most schools; however, enrollment is difficult for foreigners because German university students are faced with tightened admissions requirements. Many are being turned away due to lack of facilities.

Universities are an excellent source for finding someone with whom to exchange practice in German and English. There will probably also be a large number of German students who have studied in English-speaking countries and who may be delighted to brush up on their English skills or just meet a family from the country where they studied. If you have teenagers, inviting English-speaking German students to your home can create a bridge for your young people into university student circles and perhaps launch them into a lifelong friendship.

Among the many students from other countries at the universities in Germany, you can find many English speakers who are eager to make friends—to practice their English or to have access to home life (students can be lonely and homesick).

# 9

# Cars and Driving

Nearly everyone has heard of Germany's famous autobahns, where drivers push their cars to breakneck speeds, but a lot of people who visit Germany are not aware of the many other scenic highways with reasonable speed limits. The basic regulations regarding speed limits are 50 km/h (30 mph) in cities, 100 km/h (60 mph) on country roads and scenic highways, and no limit on autobahns. If no speed limit is posted, don't be fooled into thinking there is no limit—the limit is 50 km/h! In spite of set limits, it is always wise to let the weather, traffic, and road conditions determine when lower speeds are appropriate.

Driving is on the right, and road signs follow the international system. Drive and walk with extreme caution in Germany. The accident rate is so high that the government is clamping down severely on speeding and drunken driving. Speeders, if caught, must pay stiff fines, and drunken driving may result in imprisonment along with fines. The death toll has been appalling—50 percent more deaths per capita on the road than in Britain and 150 percent more than in the U.S.

For information about speed traps, fines, and regulations, consult Shell's *German Road Atlas* or *Europa Touring*, the AAA guide to driving in Europe. You are, for example, required to keep seatbelts fastened in an auto. A folder, entitled "Autobahn Service," shows the entire autobahn system and the location of service facilities and is available in English at roadhouses, service stations, and border crossings.

## THE BIG QUESTION: TO IMPORT OR BUY LOCALLY?

You will most likely want to own a car during your stay in Germany, not only for your exploration of Germany but for traveling throughout Europe. This poses an immediate question: is it better to import your current  car (owned three months or more) into Germany or to buy a German car?

For most people, importing a car is the less desirable choice for several reasons: import duties, the high cost of gasoline and insurance for large cars, difficulty with repairs, limited resale possibilities, and the higher annual road tax levied on American cars. If you are a tourist, you can import a car free of import duties and taxes for one year, but you must take it out of Germany at the end of that time or its status is changed and taxes imposed. Import tax based on the size and capacity of the engine must then be paid, in addition to a "turnover" tax, which is a percentage of the import tax. If you are living and working in Germany, you will have to pay the assessed customs duty, in the form of a deposit. Your car will be under customs supervision for a period of up to two years. When you leave Germany, or at the end of two years, this deposit will be returned to you. Should you want to sell the car you have imported, the regulations with which you must comply are strict and involved, and the fees you must pay are high.

All imported cars (belonging to those planning to live in Germany more than one year) must be inspected by the German Technical Inspection Team (*Technischer Uberwachungsverein* or TUV). This is done immediately after arrival to assure roadworthiness and again after two years. Imported cars must also undergo certain modifications to conform to existing German laws; the cost for these alterations can vary from U.S.$70 to $450, depending on the condition and age of the car. Americans living in Europe advise that, if you do decide to import a car, select a recent, small to midsized model and not a large V8 American car with low gas mileage.

If you buy a car in Germany, your savings may be considerable, especially if you drive it locally before shipping it home on your return. There are time restrictions, however, so investigate the laws carefully. By buying locally, you will also avoid import duties and taxes, expensive alterations to meet German requirements, and the hassle of trying to sell an imported car before you leave. Should you choose this alternative, you will be given export papers at the time you take delivery of the car. These papers must remain in your possession until you deliver the car to a shipping agent for its export to your home country. If you return a copy of the export papers to the original dealer, stamped by the German customs officials at the time of the car's export, you will recover the value-added tax (*Mehrwertsteuer*) included in the original price paid for the vehicle.

## Renting a Car

If your stay in Germany will be a short one, or if you will be living in an urban area with adequate public transportation, renting a car may be a viable option. There is no lack of reliable rental firms. Among them are Hertz, Avis, Autohansa, Auto Sixt, and Europa Service. Rental costs vary according to the size and make of the car; mileage and gasoline are extra. If you are eligible for a discounted rate at home, be sure to inquire at the German rental agency—it might apply in Germany also.

## REGULATIONS

A valid German driver's license is necessary for driving in Germany. If you produce a U.S. license, which is valid for at least twelve months from your date of arrival, you can get a German license when registering your car. Otherwise, you may have to attend a German driving school which costs about DM 600. To get your

German license, you must be at least eighteen years of age and be able to furnish passport-sized photographs and a German translation of your license. Whether or not you plan to get a German driver's license, you should renew your U.S. license prior to your departure. You should also get an international driver's license, which may be obtained from any motor club in the U.S. This, accompanied by your valid U.S. license, permits you to drive, temporarily, throughout the world. If you will be living and driving your own car in Germany, you must also have a German license.

You will have to carry third-party liability insurance (*Haftpflichtversicherung*). This is arranged through a German insurance company. A statement from your home insurance company attesting to your accident-free driving record may greatly reduce your insurance premium in Germany. The premium will be based on your driving record and on the car's horsepower. You will also need to provide proof of car ownership and of registration (if the car is imported). A motor vehicle cannot be operated in Germany until it is registered by the *Strassenverkehrsamt,* the equivalent of the Department of Motor Vehicles. The applicant must pay a motor vehicle tax (road tax) and provide proof of liability insurance and vehicle inspection.

If you plan to drive outside of Germany, you must have a nationality plate on the car and an international license. Information and regulations about international driving are readily available at any of the German auto clubs. For this reason (and many others), joining an auto club makes sense. If you are a member of a branch of the AAA, some services may be available to you from European auto clubs.

## GERMAN AUTO CLUBS

German auto clubs operate highway patrols and provide free service on all major highways for their members. The three auto clubs in Germany are as follows:

1. ADAC: Allgemeiner Deutscher Automobil Club, D 8 München 22, Königstrasse 9-11A

2. AVD:  Automobilclub von Deutschland, D 6 Frankfurt-Niederrad, Lyonerstrasse 16

3. DTC:  Deutscher Touring Automobil Club, D 8 München 60, Elisabethstrasse 30

Nonmembers may use their services but must pay a fee. ADAC (one of the larger organizations) also provides this service within major cities and operates rental services for tire chains in the mountain areas. It publishes an annual detailed camping guide as well.

# 10

# Adult Leisure

## MEETING GERMANS

It is possible to live in Germany as if you had never left home, but you will return home with few new experiences, and you will miss an opportunity for personal enrichment and real contact with a rich and wonderful culture and warm, friendly people. Meeting Germans is not difficult, but it will take some effort on your part and it is necessary to work at learning and using their language.

There are numerous ways to meet Germans informally; approachable and easygoing, they will wait for you to take the initiative rather than intruding on you. The more you try to speak German, the easier meeting Germans will be. Everyone will nod and smile and give you an encouraging "*ja, ja, ja*" as you struggle to get out a sentence. It is important to remember that while only a little initiative is necessary for meeting and becoming acquainted, a considerable amount of time and effort go into establishing a friendship.

Take part in sports; join in when there are festivals; drink beer in *Ratskeller*—sit at the long tables with others and join in the songs, even if you only hum along; talk to and ask informed questions of people you meet in parks, at museums, and on trips. Many lifelong friendships between Americans and Germans have begun on sightseeing buses, trains, and at country inns.

If you feel more comfortable with a more structured approach, you can meet Germans through a number of organizations.

***Amerika Häuser*** (German-American Clubs) are jointly sponsored by the U.S. and German governments. Though primarily concerned with introducing Germans to American culture (through lectures, films, etc.), they are excellent places for Americans and Germans to meet while attending lectures or going on trips together. Generally, language instruction in both German and English is offered at a reasonable cost. Inquire also about the Goethe Institute programs, publications, films, and the monthly *German Review* of social and political topics.

Amerika Häuser are located in Berlin, Köln, Frankfurt, Freiburg, Hamburg, Hanover, Heidelberg, München, Nürnberg, Regensberg, Saarbrücken, Stuttgart, and Tübingen.

**"Meet the Germans"** is a program sponsored by the Association of German-American Clubs. The activities of these groups, operating under the umbrella of the Federation of German-American Clubs, are more social in nature than those of Amerika Häuser. They, and their parent organization, are actively involved in sponsoring student exchange programs. You may want to write to the Federation of German-American Clubs (7 Stuttgart, Richard Wagnerstrasse 14) for the name of the German-American Club in your new city and make an initial contact by mail. This will alert the group's newcomer welcome committee to your arrival, making your early days far more pleasant.

***Atlantik Brücke*** (Atlantic Bridge, 2000 Hamburg 65, Sanderskoppel 15) is an organization devoted to introducing people with the same interest or profession. The Atlantik Brücke in Hamburg holds interesting "counterpart" meetings, by profession, which you are welcome to attend.

***Amerikanische Gesselschaft in Deutschland*** (2 Hamburg 13, Testdorpfstrasse 1) arranges meetings between groups and gives advice to American travelers.

There are also Rotary and Lions clubs throughout Germany; check with your clubs at home for German counterparts. American-

German chambers of commerce in many cities also have gatherings for businesspeople.

You will also make acquaintances and connections through participation in the activities of your children's schools and scout troops or your church.

If you are a university graduate, you may want to get in touch with the University Graduates Club (men) or the Association of University Women. These groups bring together people from many cultures, who meet to hear interesting speakers and to participate in organized trips. American women can join the American Association of University Women before leaving home so that on arrival, they will already have an affiliation with the group. For information write AAUW, 2401 Virginia Avenue, NW, Washington, DC 20037.

If you move to a large city where there is a consulate or embassy, you should drop in, pay your respects, and make your presence known. The embassy or consulate is often a good source of information about activities or channels through which you can meet local people. Don't expect a great deal of assistance, however, since the consulates are not prepared to provide services for expatriates.

## WORK FOR AMERICAN SPOUSES

One question expatriate spouses frequently ask is, "Can I work?" In order to hold most jobs, you must have a work permit, and to get a permit, you must be able to speak German. However, if your German is less than fluent and you cannot obtain a work permit, there are other options available. One possibility worth exploring is giving lessons in English (or other languages), piano, aerobics, flower arranging, or carpentry at home. Many spouses who cannot qualify for a work permit occupy their time profitably by sharing their talents with others.

A second option is teaching in American and/or international schools. For more information contact the following agencies:

U.S. Department of Defense, Washington, DC 20301

Directorate, U.S. Dependents Schools, European Area, 75 Karlsruhe, Germany

Office of Overseas Schools, U.S. State Department, Washington, DC 20520

College Placement, Inc., 35 E. Elizabeth Avenue, Bethlehem, PA 18018 (also has placement listings for overseas business and government posts)

International Schools Service, 126 Alexander Street, Princeton, NJ 08540

Finally, you may want to pursue the option of working for the U.S. government or for an American business. Sources of information include

Business:

*Directory of American Business* in Germany (available in commercial libraries), Seibt-Verlag, 8 München 8, Anzinger Strasse 1

U.S. military:

Director Civilian Personnel Office, Frankfurt/Main, Hansa Alle 24-26

Nursing positions in U.S. military hospitals:

Surgeon General's Office, U.S. Army, 69 Heidelberg

## SPORTS

The Germans are an athletic and vigorous people. All kinds of sports activities are popular and readily available. Camping, biking, and hiking are long-standing favorites, and so are the many different kinds of mechanized racing. Germans love speed and turn out in droves for car, motorbike, speedboat, or bicycle racing.

Other popular sports include polo, tennis, ice hockey, gliding, and horse racing. Another popular sport is fencing, and Germany is a wonderful place to learn it because the Germans are among the world's best fencers. Skiing and ice-skating are winter favorites; there are some three hundred ski resorts in Germany alone, not to mention those in Switzerland, France, or Scandinavia, all easily reached by short plane or pleasant train rides.

**Hosteling.** Germany is well known for its youth hostels, 750 of which dot the landscape. Many are in historic castles and monasteries. Walking or riding a bicycle from one hostel to another along the old roads, canals, or rivers is an experience to be savored. And anyone can do it—from teenagers to the young at heart. It is an excellent way to experience Germany, to meet a cross section of Europeans, and to make new friends. For further information contact Deutsches Jugendherbergswerk, D-493 Detmold, Bülow-strasse 26; or American Youth Hostels, 1332 Eye Street NW, Suite 800, Washington, DC 20005.

**Golf.** A guide to Germany's golf courses is published each year in German by Golf und Sportverlag, Horst Ostermann, D 6202 Wiesbaden-Bieberich, Rudolf-Vogt-Strasse 1.

**Sailing.** Germany's many lakes and hundreds of miles of coast make it ideal for sailing, and lessons for the novice are readily available. For information contact the German Yachting Association, D 2 Hamburg 22, Schwanenwik 27. Another useful address is Verband Deutscher Segelschulen, D 44 Münster, Bottshaus am Aasee. If you are a sailing buff, be sure not to miss the big Regatta Week each year at Kiel.

**Fishing.** Lake, river, stream, and deep-sea fishing are available, but you will need two licenses: state and owner's. For information contact Verband Deutscher Sportfischer, D 605 Offenbach, Waldstrasse 6.

**Hiking and Climbing.** The Verband Deutscher Gebirgs und Wandervereine (Germany's chief hiking and climbing organization) is composed of forty-seven clubs with two thousand local chapters and three hundred thousand members. Contact the organization for more information: D 7 Stuttgart, Hospitalstrasse 21 b.

The German Alpine Association operates 239 huts, which are open to all climbers; members receive a 50 percent discount. The association's address is Alpenvereinshaus, D 8 München, 5 Prater-insel, 22.

**Walking.** If you enjoy walking, the *Volksmarch* will delight you. The Volksmarch is an organized walk along a marked trail that may skirt private yards, cut through farms, follow forest paths, or meander along village streets—often all of the above. There are control points (*Kontrolle*), where you will receive light refresh-ments (practically a full meal) and a progress stamp on your pass. The final stamp is available at the finish (*Ziel*). The rates are reasonable, and the walks offer a unique view of the countryside and of the Germans.

The German National Association (DVV) is an umbrella organ-ization for the over 1,700 separate "wandering" clubs. Altogether, these clubs sponsor as many as 1,600 Volksmarch events each year. Joining a club will insure that you receive a calendar of events, record books, and other materials. For more information, contact DVV-Geschäftsstelle, 8262 Altötting, Fabrikstrasse 8.

**Flying.** If flying is your sport, you will find ample opportunity to take to the skies. The Aero Club, at D 6 Frankfurt, Lyonerstrasse 16, has a thousand chapters. A listing of flying schools is available from the German Tourist Office in any major city.

## THE ARTS

**Theater.** The Germans love theater and support some 190 active theaters in approximately four hundred cities and towns, some of which are run for and by workers in connection with trade unions. No matter where you are in Germany, you will probably be within fifty miles of a theater, where a wide range of the world's great dramas—Russian, Italian, British, Irish, American, ancient Greek, and prize-winning German works—are being presented. In the summer, dramas are presented in spectacular outdoor settings. In fact, theater may be your greatest incentive for learning the German language. Curtain time at most theaters is 2000, sometimes earlier. Tickets normally go on sale ten days in advance of the opening, starting on a Saturday, and may be purchased at ticket offices at various locations in the larger cities as well as at theater box offices. The hotel concierge is often a good source of information about tickets.

**Movies.** Movie production is relatively new for Germany; even so, German directors are producing fine films whose quality is recognized throughout the world. Many U.S. and British films are shown with German sound tracks or subtitles—an ideal way to practice the language. There is also an interesting selection of films from Italy, Sweden, Czechoslovakia, and other countries.

**Music.** Germans are especially fond of music. Every major city has its own philharmonic orchestra, and sixty-three cities have permanent opera and ballet companies. Annual festivals abound; some of the best known are at Bayreuth, München, Berlin, and Wiesbaden. Popular operetta is performed from the end of June to mid-September on a floating stage at Koblenz. All in all, there is music for all tastes. To make sure you don't miss your favorites, get a calendar of events from the nearest German Tourist Office.

**Miscellaneous.** If you have never lived abroad before, you may not realize that reading is an important pastime. Although English-language books can be obtained (at a high price), the selection may not meet your interests. You can order books from catalogues, and you may want to join a book club before leaving home to insure a steady supply of reading material.

If you enjoy do-it-yourself projects, you will find excellent tools at your disposal. Gardening is very popular among the Germans and supplies are abundant. If music is your hobby, you will find musical instruments for rent at moderate prices. There is very little, in fact, that you cannot find to help you pursue those activities that you enjoy or have always wanted to learn or try.

# TRAVEL

For the real flavor of Germany and German hospitality, stop at a hostel, guesthouse (*Gasthaus*), or inn when you travel. You may find yourself staying in a converted castle, a chapel, a timbered inn, or a medieval monastery. Picturesque, comfortable, clean, inexpensive, and delightful, these low-cost accommodations are a bargain, and meals are included. If you don't want to plan your accommodations in advance, an accommodation bureau (*Zimmernachweis*), located at every railroad station and airport in Germany, can help you find local hotels with vacancies.

Wherever you decide to stay, be it a hotel, inn, manor house, hotel, or pension, you will find that rooms with private baths are about 50 percent higher than rooms without. This goes for most of the rest of Europe as well. Always take your own washcloths and soap as these are considered as personal as toothbrushes and are rarely supplied (even in private homes). The smart European tourist also carries toilet paper since many public restrooms are not equipped with it.

If you prefer to travel the *autobahns,* you will find good restaurants and motels along the way as well as emergency telephones every mile or so.

One thing you will notice when traveling in Germany is the special clothing seen in villages during local festivals. The clothing is often particular to specific locales; for example, *Lederhosen* and *Dirndl* dresses, usually considered typically German, are really Bavarian. These and other colorful, often very elaborate, costumes will most likely appear at events such as *Karnival, Fasching* (pre-Lenten celebrations), or local festivals.

**Camping.** Camping is almost a national sport. If you are interested, get the official guide of the Deutscher Camping Club, which is called *Campingführer.* This guide lists some three thousand camping sites in Germany and twenty other countries. Filled with quantities of information, including symbols explained in English, it is available at bookstores and sporting goods shops or you can order it directly from Deutscher Camping Club e.V., 8 München 23, Mandelstrasse 28.

# 11

# Major Cities

## BREMEN/BREMERHAVEN

Located at the end of the Weser Estuary, Bremen is the oldest maritime city in Germany; it was a key international trading port in the fifteenth century. Still one of the world's greatest ports, Bremen handles about 10 percent of Germany's foreign trade. Most of its working population is employed either in port-connected jobs (40 percent) or in industry.

Bremerhaven, thirty-seven miles downstream, was founded in 1827 as a deep-sea port for Bremen. Together they form an outstanding commercial port system—half the German fishing fleet is based in Bremerhaven.

## Housing

The newest section of Bremen lies on the west bank of the river. It is extremely modern, with large apartment blocks and shopping centers. Just beyond the old city, to the east, is the new satellite town of Neue Vahr. Its apartment houses, broad boulevards, and modern office buildings give it a contemporary and welcoming atmosphere. Commuter transportation from these suburban areas is good. As in most German cities, housing is scarce and difficult to locate, so it may take quite some time to find a place to live.

## Leisure Activities

You will not suffer from a lack of interesting activities during your stay in this area. All water sports are popular, and various international yachting regattas are held here. You will find several golf courses; indoor and outdoor tennis and swimming facilities, many of which are open to the public; riding clubs; soccer clubs; and both fishing and hunting (bear, deer, hare, duck, and geese). Bremen's six-day bicycle race is world-famous.

Spend time exploring the old town of Bremen on the east bank of the Weser, where you will discover what was once a walled city in the Middle Ages. You can still see the location of the moat that once surrounded the city, now an attractive park that includes Rampart Walk. One old street (a street of crafts even long ago) called Bottcherstrasse is filled with galleries and practicing crafts-people. Throughout the year the Stadthalle offers high quality shows featuring internationally known stars. Several museums and galleries are noteworthy: (1) the Übersee Museum, famous for its demon-strations of the various skills and crafts of the peoples of northern Germany; (2) the Focke Museum, specializing in the rich history of the region; (3) the Kunsthalle, featuring a remarkable collection of nineteenth- and twentieth-century German and French art; and (4) the National Maritime Museum in Bremerhaven, which traces German maritime history from its beginnings. During the summer, visitors may explore seven ships moored at an open-air exhibit, which is part of the Maritime Museum.

Short trips to the surrounding countryside will take you to prehistoric Wildeshausen; the artist colony of Worpswede; sunny, though chilly, Cuxhaven beach; the upper Weser River or the North Sea for fishing; and the Harz Mountains for skiing.

## Clothes

Cold, damp, and windy sums up Bremen's weather, so wool or other heavy, warm clothing is essential: warm slacks, sweaters, suits, windbreakers, coats, and boots. Warm nightclothes and underwear are a necessity. Since the Germans economize on heating fuel (which has become astronomically expensive in Europe), you will find bedrooms and hallways cooler than individual offices and those rooms in homes used by the entire family during the day. Because of this, dressing so that you can add or remove clothing (layering) is both practical and commonplace.

## Some Useful Addresses

U.S. Consulate-General, 28 Bremen, 1 President-Kennedy-Platz

Bremen Tourist Association (Verkehrsverein Bremen), Tivoli-Hochhaus, Bahnhofsplatz 29

# DÜSSELDORF

Düsseldorf is the busiest port on the Rhine, a center for East-West trade and transport, and its airport is one of the busiest in Europe. Some seven hundred thousand people live in the city; a total of nine million live within fifty kilometers. There is a constant flow of tourists and visitors. In spite of this, the city maintains a small-town feeling. Düsseldorf is a city for people—lively and full of activity—yet it offers an open, relaxed atmosphere that is unusual for a city its size. This pleasant atmosphere is due partly to the Rhine River, which flows through the middle of town, and partly to its extensive parks, like the Hofgarten, and its stately boulevards. Careful planning has preserved the residential character of the city while allowing for industrial expansion.

Known as the "desk of the Ruhr," Düsseldorf boasts the second largest stock exchange in Germany, houses over five hundred commercial institutions, and served as a major banking center long before the Rothschilds opened their first offices there. Over forty-four countries maintain consulates in Düsseldorf, and it is the site of Japan's largest overseas trade center. A trade fair of some sort is almost always in process at the enormous complex on the northern edge of the city.

The city melds old and new ideas rather easily in a cosmopolitan setting. Because it was a vital port area, the city was heavily damaged during World War II, and it looks like a new city due to massive postwar reconstruction. As the capital of North Rhine-Westphalia, it is the location of the State Parliament. It is also a university town with a new campus, built in 1965, drawing many young people to the city. A leader in the arts, Düsseldorf attracts many artists—actors, filmmakers, musicians, painters, and fashion designers. A city with a diverse population, nearly half of its residents (46 percent) have come from other cities or countries in the past twenty-five years. The annual Düsseldorf fashion show is said to be the largest in the world, and the city is a shopper's paradise. The Germans call it *die heitere Stadt* (the happy city), and it is indeed a city to enjoy.

## Leisure Activities

Sports activities and facilities are numerous: indoor and outdoor tennis courts (hard courts at the Rhine Stadium, which has many facilities for sports), skating and ice-hockey rinks, swimming and fishing at nearby Lake Unterback, riding schools, polo clubs, eighteen-hole golf courses, soccer, bowling, billiards, and boccie (a game of Italian origin similar to lawn bowling) are among those from which you may choose.

At the heart of Düsseldorf is the Königsallee (the "Ko"), which follows a portion of the moat that once surrounded the old town. Along the Ko are cafés, restaurants, luxury shops, and a great deal of activity. The Ko leads to the Hofgarten, a lovely park with a number of charming fountains. You can stroll in the old town or visit the many fine museums located here. The Rhineland-Westphalia Collection at the Jägerhof Castle includes works by the twentieth-century artists Klee, Chagall, Kandinsky, and Picasso. The Goethe Museum displays pictures of the writer as well as first editions of his works and other memorabilia. Trips along the Rhine are popular, as are the drives to ancient castles, such as the Chateau of Dyck and the Chateau of Rheydt.

## Some Useful Addresses

U.S. Consulate General, 4000 Düsseldorf, Cecillenalle 5

American Chamber of Commerce, Gunter Mayer Rolshofen, 4000 Düsseldorf, Wirmerstrasse 11

Anglo-German Society, Witthaurer, Duisburgerstrasse 11a

Chamber of Industry and Commerce in Düsseldorf, Berliner Allee 10

Tourist and Trade Promotion Office, Ehrenhof 3

Association of Cultural Organizations, Heinrich Heine Allee 49-51

The Brucke-International Educational Center (School for Extra-mural Studies), Heinrich Heine Allee 49-51

Youth Hostel, Düsseldorfstrasse 1

## FRANKFURT AM MAIN

Cosmopolitan Frankfurt is a modern, prosperous city with a population of about 700,000 and a history dating from A.D. 834 Unfortunately, the old city is now only a small, largely reconstructed area around the Romerberg Square. Here you will find the Romer, with fifteenth-century burghers' houses, the Baroque Sallhof (once an imperial palace), and other historic sites. Frankfurt's cathedral (*Dom*) has played an important role in German history as far back as the Holy Roman Empire. German emperors were crowned in the cathedral for many centuries.

Because of its central location, Frankfurt is a huge transportation junction for air traffic (third largest airport in Europe), railway and road traffic, and autobahns which converge here from every direction.

Frankfurt also has the distinction of being the financial and commercial capital of the Federal Republic. The Frankfurt Stock

Exchange, which leads all others in Germany, is located at Borsenplatz, together with the Chamber of Industry and Commerce and many trade organizations. Frankfurt hosts trade fairs, book fairs, and industrial exhibitions in huge numbers. The Exhibition Grounds cover 360,000 square meters and house modern exhibition centers, foreign pavilions, the Congress Hall, and the Festival Hall.

No European city has shaped itself so much in the American image as Frankfurt. Largely rebuilt after World War II, its skyscrapers, subways, and supermarkets mirror those of American cities. Local residents, though, are not entirely satisfied with their American-style city and regret the loss of its German identity.

## Housing

Situated on both sides of the Main River, Frankfurt offers a variety of neighborhoods and lifestyles to newcomers.

Residential areas north of the river receive high ratings from foreign residents. Accommodations range from three-room apartments with kitchen and bath to two-story townhouses and luxury bungalows. There is generally a larger selection of homes here than elsewhere in the city. Rents, however, are no different from those in the rest of Frankfurt—high. Connections to the city are excellent: U-bahn, bus, and streetcar. In fact, transportation throughout Frankfurt is good.

South of the river, the area of Niederrad is appealing because of convenient connections to the autobahns and Frankfurt International Airport. For relaxation there are peaceful wooded areas, Frankfurt's only golf course, the race track, a big league soccer stadium, and plenty of paths for walking the dog or jogging. Bordering Niederrad is Sachsenhausen; its colorful apple wine festivals and flea markets make it an enjoyable spot to visit.

Frankfurt's 155,000 commuters, many of them expatriates, find the train service excellent and the rents between 10 and 15 percent lower in the outlying suburbs. Among choice locations are Wiesbaden, Darmstadt, and Oberursel. Besides offering a more relaxed pace, the suburbs are the location of the American and international schools: U.S. Defense Department (DOD) schools in Wiesbaden and Darmstadt and the independent, private Frankfurt International School in Oberursel. There are also three U.S. Department of Defense elementary schools, one high school, and one junior high school in the northern part of Frankfurt.

Shopping centers have sprung up in strategic locations for the convenience of suburban shoppers. One is the Taunus Zentrum, southwest of Wiesbaden, just off the autobahn in the suburb of Höchst. Another great attraction in the otherwise industrial Höchst is Jahrhunderthalle (Century Hall), which draws renowned performers in both classical and contemporary theater and all kinds of music.

## Leisure Activities

Frankfurters are rightfully proud of their parks, especially the Stadtwald, a wooded area covering almost 11,000 acres within the city limits—a lovely area for children and adults alike. Within the Stadtwald is the Waldstadium, a track for cyclists, a swimming pool, tennis courts, an ice-skating rink, and various sports halls. The Frankfurt Zoo is world-famous, known for its rare species and natural animal habitats.

The city operates a number of theaters and the Opera House. Its wholesale market (Ruckerstrasse 6) is one of the largest in Europe, a source of the freshest fruits, vegetables, and flowers. The Senckenberg Museum houses a remarkable paleontology collection, and Stadel Museum is famous for its Flemish Primitive and sixteenth-century German paintings. Frankfurt is the birthplace of Goethe. His home, reconstructed after the war, and the adjoining Goethe Museum are open to the public.

Since Frankfurt is a major transportation hub, it is easy to travel northwest to places like the vacation town of Rudesheim, the charming city of Koblentz, and Köln, with its magnificent cathedral. You can take a delightful cruise along the Rhine, viewing the castles, vineyards, and villages along its shores. To the north lies Kassel, with the Hercules statue towering over the park, fountains, and the Chateau of Wilhelmshohe (now a fine museum). Also to the north is Marburg, where half-timbered houses cluster around a hill crowned by the medieval castle that dominates the town. To the south lies Heidelberg, the oldest university town in Germany and a well-known cultural center.

## Useful Addresses

U.S. Consulate, 6000 Frankfurt, Siesmayerstrasse 21; APO New York 09757*

Amerika Haus, Staufenstrasse 1

American Chamber of Commerce, Rossmarkt 12. Will provide information about local business conditions, help with forms, attorneys, stenographers, translators, etc.

German-American Club (Steuben-Schurz-Gesellschaft e.V.), 6000 Frankfurt am Main, Barckhausstrasse 18

Tourist Office, facing track 23 in the railroad station (called Frankfurter Verkehrsverein); provides information and advice in English about housing, theater, concerts, sports, local facilities, the area, baby-sitters, and almost anything; also a source for tickets to sports and cultural events

## MÜNCHEN (MUNICH)

München, the third largest city in Germany and the largest city in Bavaria, was settled by monks in the eighth century; hence, the name *München*, meaning "home of the monks." Almost 1.3 million people live in the 120-square-mile valley situated 1,700 feet above sea level. Despite its twelve-hundred-year history, München is new in many respects because so much of it had to be restored after World War II. Much of the rebuilt area is along grandiose lines, showing considerable Italian influence.

* When using an APO, do not write the German street address or city—it slows down delivery immensely.

The city is young in another sense too, for over 40 percent of its residents are under the age of thirty-five. Roughly 50,000 are students at the University of Munich, the College of Technology, the School of Fine Arts, or the Bavarian State Academy of Music. München is also home to an active international community of more than 200,000 foreigners. In addition, tourists flock there during both summer and winter to enjoy the surrounding mountains, lakes, and the Bavarian atmosphere. Many people consider it Germany's loveliest, liveliest, and most enjoyable city.

München has attracted a diversity of business but is not plagued with the soot and grime of the northern industrial cities. Instead, it is noted for beer making, electronics, vehicle construction, fashions, printing, movies, optical and precision instruments, and civil engineering. There are many banks, insurance companies, and scientific research institutes. Large commercial exhibits at the Theresienhohe feature crafts, construction machinery, and other products of the region.

You will find the people of Bavaria far more relaxed and less formal than the people of northern Germany, and they are proud of the fact. Even their dialect differs; the local greeting, for example, is *Grüss Gott* (God be with you) rather than *Guten Tag*, the greeting in most of Germany. Bavarians are enthusiastic beer drinkers, heavy eaters, and great lovers of music.

## Housing

Housing is scarce and accommodations tend to be small, as in most German cities. Most people live in large multiplex apartment buildings or in row houses. By German standards Americans live well in München, occupying many of the best-located and best-equipped apartments. The public transportation system is excellent and consists of the U-bahn, streetcar and bus service, and the S-bahn, which reaches well beyond city limits. Because this is a large metropolitan area, people tend to consider proximity to schools first (if they have school-age children) and to jobs second when searching for a place to live.

The listings of apartments and houses for rent in the Friday edition of the *Süddeutsche Zeitung* and the Saturday edition of the *Münchner Merkur* are the best resources for house or apartment hunting. Placing an ad in the apartment- or house-wanted sections of those papers is also useful.

## Leisure Activities

München is a delightful city to explore. The Marienplatz, the heart of the old city, is flanked by the new city hall with its famous *Glockenspiel* (the largest carillon in Germany) and ringed by small streets lined with luxury shops, restaurants, and cafés. The magnificent churches located here include St. Michael's and the cathedral, both restored after the war. Perhaps the most stunning, certainly the most surprising, is the Church of Our Lady. Severely damaged by bombing, the sober brick facade markedly contrasts with a dazzling white, modern nave and contemporary stained glass windows. Close by is the open market, with beautifully arranged vegetables and flowers, and a street lined with butcher shops from which hang vast quantities of *Wurst*. Of course, there are the great beer halls, the most famous of which is the Hofbrauhaus, with its many rooms and courtyards, and bands playing lively tunes.

Operas and concerts are truly outstanding, and the theater and ballet equally notable. There is a great variety of important museums and galleries. The Alte Pinakothek, with masterpieces by Rubens, Dürer, and Van Dyck, is considered one of the seven most important art galleries in the world. The Neue Pinakothek has an important collection of eighteenth- and nineteenth-century paintings and sculpture. The Deutsches Museum, which rates with the Smithsonian, features displays of scientific and technological developments from the Stone Age to the present. The Palace of the Dukes of Wittelsbach (constructed around seven courtyards) and the Palace Museum, Theater, and Opera display the glory of royal life in old München. Churches are mostly Catholic or Lutheran; the U.S. Army provides a large Sunday school and three small churches in south and central München (all of which are available to Americans).

Outdoor activities are abundant; there are two public golf courses, tennis courts, swimming pools, skating arenas, bowling centers, and riding clubs. Children enjoy the many parks and the Hellabrün Zoo. Outside München, you can learn mountain climbing in the Isar Valley, ski in Allgau and Werdenfelser, and swim, camp, and sail in the Tegernsee, with its charming small towns. The health resort of Bad Tolz is also popular. The S-bahn provides easy access to Lake Starnberg or the Ammersee Lake with Andechs Monastery, where excellent beer is brewed. It is great fun to take a picnic dinner, buy a few liters of beer, and relax in the beer hall or courtyard of Andechs.

München is a great city for celebrating and seems to host a constant round of festivals. Oktoberfest is world-renowned, and *Fasching* (carnival) features literally thousands of masked balls. The summer cultural festivities reach their high point with the Opera Festival in July; and, as one foreign resident put it, "You just haven't celebrated Christmas until you live in Munich." The city seems to glow in the winter holiday season, and the *Christkindlmarkt* on Marienplatz is a real treat for "people watchers" as well as a source of both small, inexpensive gifts and ornaments and more expensive craft items.

## Useful Addresses

U.S. Consulate-General, 8000 München 22, Königinstrasse 5

American Chamber of Commerce, 8000 München, Zweibrückenstrasse 6

Amerika Haus, 8 München, Karolinenplatz 3

Federation of German-American Clubs, 8 München 40, Birnauerstrasse 6

Verkehrsamt (Tourist Office), D-8000 München 2, Rindermarkt 5; the Tourist Office has a wealth of information about Munich and will supply useful brochures and maps and, upon request, the "Official Monthly Program" by mail

## BONN

Although it is the capital city of the Federal Republic of Germany, Bonn is among its smaller cities, with a population of less than 290,000 in its metropolitan area.

Situated twenty miles from Köln, Bonn spreads out on both banks of the Rhine River and is the gateway to the Rhine Valley. One of the oldest settlements in Germany, its history dates back 2,000 years. Under the name of Castra Bonnensia, Bonn was the site of one of the earliest Roman forts on the Rhine River and an important part of the Romans' defense of the area. It is also the site of one of the first Christian shrines, built to honor the memory of two Roman soldiers, Cassius and Florentius, who were killed because of their belief in Christianity. Today the Bonn cathedral stands on this spot.

In the thirteenth century, the archbishops of Köln established their residence in Bonn and were responsible for the  development of the city as it is today. The parks and avenues were laid out, monuments were erected, and the residence itself was constructed. The old and famous University of Bonn was completed in 1725. Also built during this period were Poppelsdorfer Schloss and the city hall. Bonn was selected as the capital of the Federal Republic of Germany in 1949.

Bad Godesberg, an ancient and well-known spa, is incorporated into the city of Bonn and houses much of the diplomatic community. It is also the birthplace of Beethoven. The house in which he was born in 1770 is now a museum.

## Schools

There are American, British, and French elementary schools in the area, all of which follow their home-country curriculum. At the elementary level, there are Catholic, Protestant, and nondenominational private schools. The Nicolas-Cusanus Gymnasium near the Plittersdorf is one of the few high schools prepared to give international students special attention. It is tuition-free and there are special German classes designed to help international students learn the language.

## Leisure Activities

Bonn is a bustling city—a combination of political, intellectual, cultural, and commercial activities abound. Its operas, plays, concerts, and festivals are among the best in the country. During *Bonner Sommer*, from the beginning of May through September, concerts, drama, and dance are performed on stages in the Markt Platz, the Gartenschau Park, and the Pavillon in Bad Godesberg. Summer is also the time for concerts at Schloss Bruhl in Köln and in the courtyard of the Poppelsdorfer Schloss.

At the end of summer, wine festivals celebrate the grape harvest. Each village has its own festival featuring dancing to the music of local bands, contests, and, most important, wine tasting of last year's local vintage.

Children from two to ninety-two will enjoy the Christkindlmarkt in Münster Platz. From late November until Christmas it features booths full of sweets, wooden ornaments, and handcrafts. It is a great source of small and inexpensive gifts.

Religious services are conducted in English at the St. Boniface Anglican Episcopal Church and at the Christian Science Church. Protestant, Catholic, and Jewish services are available in German.

Activity and enrichment groups exist for almost every age group and every interest. The *Bonn Journal* is the best source of information on the activities of the various groups as well as for information on concerts, art exhibits, and special events.

# 12

# Sources of Information

**IN THE U.S.A.**

**Government**

Embassy of the Federal Republic of Germany, 4645 Reservoir Road NW, Washington, DC 20007. Tel: (202) 298-4000.

German Consulate General, 601 California Street, New York, NY 10022. Tel: (212) 308-8700. Offices are also located in Atlanta, Boston, Chicago, Cleveland, Detroit, Houston, Los Angeles, Miami, San Francisco, and Seattle.

German Information Center, 950 Third Avenue, New York, NY 10022. Tel: (212) 888-9840.

German National Tourist Office, 747 Third Avenue, New York, NY 10017. Tel: (212) 308-3300; 444 South Flower, Los Angeles, CA. Tel: (213) 688-7332.

Goethe Institutes in the U.S. The ten U.S. branches of the Goethe Institute of Munich strive to provide information about Germany and strengthen the cultural ties between Germany and the U.S. by providing information about Germany and by offering language courses. Additionally, they organize and sponsor a variety

**113**

of cultural events in cooperation with a variety of American institutions. Goethe Institutes are located in Ann Arbor, Atlanta, Boston, Chicago, Houston, Los Angeles, New York, St. Louis, San Francisco, and Seattle.

U.S. Commerce Department, Country Specialist for the Federal Republic of Germany, 14th and Constitution Avenue NW, Room 3409, Washington, DC 20230. Tel: (202) 377-2434; or the nearest field office.

U.S. State Department, Country Specialist for the Federal Republic of Germany, 2201 C Street NW, Room 4228, Washington, DC 20520-6511. Tel: (202) 647-2155.

## Nongovernment

American Council on Germany, 99 Park Avenue, New York, NY 10016. Tel: (212) 826-3636 (see local phone listings for convenient locations).

German-American Chamber of Commerce, 666 Fifth Avenue, New York, NY 10103. Tel: (212) 974-8830. Offices are also located in Washington, D.C., Chicago, Los Angeles, San Francisco, Atlanta, and Houston. Publishes monthly *German American Trade News,* annual *American Subsidiaries of German Firms*, and statistical and trade summaries.

## IN GERMANY

## Government

Amerika Haus. Sponsored by the German and U.S. governments, Amerika Haus has branches in Berlin, Köln, Frankfurt, Freiburg, Hamburg, Hannover, Heidelberg, München, Nürnberg, Regensberg, Saarbrücken, Stuttgart, and Tübingen. Inquire about programs, various publications, language classes, films, and the monthly *German Review* of social and political topics.

German Center for Tourism, 6000 Frankfurt am Main 1, Beethov-
enstrasse 69. Branch offices are located in most cities and large
towns.

Goethe Institute of Munich. The fifteen branches of the Goethe Institute in Germany offer courses in German for daily use and for
specific purposes.

Institute for Foreign Relations (Institut für Auslandsbeziehungen),
7 Stuttgart 1, Charlottenplatz 17. This organization provides information and two- and three-week professional seminars on the
people, education, history, and culture of Germany and the
Germans.

U.S. Embassy, 5300 Bonn 2, Deichmanns Avenue (APO New York
09080).*

U.S. Consulates and Commercial Offices:
 Berlin: D-1000 Berlin 33 (Dahlem), Clayallee 170 (APO New York
  09742).
 Düsseldorf: 4000 Düsseldorf 11, Emmanuel-Leutze Strasse 1B
  (APO New York 90842).
 Frankfurt am Main: 6000 Frankfurt, Siesmayerstrasse 21 (APO
  New York 09213).
 Hamburg: 2000 Hamburg 36, Alsterufer 27-28 (APO New York
  09215-0002).
 München: 8000 München 22, Koeniginstrasse 5 (APO New York
  09108).
 Stuttgart: 7000 Stuttgart, Urbanstrasse 7 (APO New York 09154).

## Nongovernment

American Chamber of Commerce in Germany, 6000 Frankfurt am
Main, Rossmarkt 12, with offices also in Bremen, Berlin, Düsseldorf, and München.

* When mailing from the U.S., use the APO only, to expedite delivery. From outside
the U.S., use the street address.

# 13

# Recommended Reading

## GENERAL

Barzini, Luigi. *The Europeans.* New York: Simon & Schuster, 1983.

Burmeister, Irmgard, ed. *Meet Germany.* Hamburg, West Germany: Atlantik Brücke (Atlantic Bridge), 1980.

Burmeister, Irmgard. *These Strange German Ways.* 14th ed. Hamburg: Atlantik Brücke, 1980.

Craig, Gordon A. *The German.* New York: Putnam, 1982.

Detwiler, Donald S. *Germany: A Short History.* Carbondale, IL: Southern Illinois State University, 1976.

Dornberg, John. *The New Germans.* New York: Macmillan, 1975.

*Fodors Guide to Germany 1989.* New York: McKay, 1989.

Hass, Ernst. *In Germany.* New York: Viking Press, 1977.

Huber, Heinz. *Haven't We Met Before Somewhere?* Illustrated by Ronald Searle. New York: Viking Press, 1966.

Kloss, Gunther. *West Germany: An Introduction.* New York: Halstead, 1976.

Kohls, L. Robert. *Survival Kit for Overseas Living*, 2nd ed. Yarmouth, ME: Intercultural Press, Inc., 1984.

Kramer, Dieter. *German Holidays and Folk Customs.* Hamburg: Atlantik Brücke, 1981.

Kramer, Jane. "Letter from West Germany." *New Yorker*, 19 December 1983.

Larson, Bob. *Getting Along with the Germans.* Esslingen am Neckar: Verlag Bechtle Esslingen, 1983.

Lewis, Flora. *Europe: A Tapestry of Nations.* New York: Simon & Schuster, 1987.

Noelle-Neumann, Elisabeth. *The Germans: Public Opinion Polls, 1967-1980.* Westport, CT and London: Greenwood Press, 1981.

Peck, Reginald. *West Germans: How They Live and Work.* New York: Praeger, 1977.

Steiner, Shari. *The Female Factor: Women in Western Europe.* Yarmouth, ME: Intercultural Press, Inc., 1982.

Von Staden, Wendelgard. *Darkness over the Valley: Growing Up in Nazi Germany.* New York: Ticknor & Fields, 1981.

## BUSINESS AND ECONOMICS

Anders, George. "Executive Style: Bosses in West Germany Stress Consensus Decision, Technical Know-How." *Wall Street Journal*, 25 September 1984.

Copeland, Lennie, and Lewis Griggs. *Going International: How to Make Friends and Deal Effectively in the Global Marketplace.* New York: New American Library, Penguin, Inc., 1985.

Cullingford, C. C. *Trade Unions in West Germany.* Boulder, CO: Westview Press, 1977.

*Doing Business in Germany.* Price-Waterhouse, New York (updated regularly).

Drucker, Peter F. "What We Can Learn from the Germans." *Wall Street Journal,* 6 March 1986.

Ernst and Ernst. *West Germany: International Business Series.* New York (updated regularly).

*Germany: Business Study.* Touche Ross International. New York (updated regularly).

Hall, Edward T., and Mildred Hall. *Understanding Cultural Differences: Germans, French and Americans.* Yarmouth, ME: Intercultural Press, Inc., 1990.

Harris, Philip R., and Robert T. Moran. *Managing Cultural Differences.* Houston: Gulf Publishing Co., 1987.

Romer, Karl, ed. *Facts about Germany.* Press and Information Office of the Federal Republic of Germany, 1985, revised 1988.

Schmidt, Klaus D. *Doing Business in the Federal Republic of Germany.* San Francisco: SRI International, 1988.

Turner, Henry Ashby, Jr. *German Big Business and the Rise of Hitler.* New York: Oxford University Press, 1985.

## GOVERNMENT AND POLITICS

Ardagh, John. *Germany and the Germans—an Anatomy of Society Today.* New York: Harper & Row, 1987.

Baker, Kendall L., Russell J. Dalton, and Kai Hildebrandt. *Germany Transformed.* Boston: Harvard University Press, 1981.

Burdick, Charles, ed. *Contemporary Germany: Politics & Culture.* Boulder, CO: Westview Press, 1984.

Carr, Jonathan. *Helmut Schmidt: Helmsman of Germany.* New York: St. Martin's Press, 1985.

Edinger, Lewis J. *West German Politics.* New York: Columbia University Press, 1986.

Gress, David. *Peace and Survival: West Germany, the Peace Movement and Security.* Stanford, CA: Hoover Institution, Stanford University Press, 1985.

Johnson, Nevil. *Government in the Federal Republic of Germany: The Executive at Work.* Elmsford, NY: Pergamon Press, 1974.

Merrit, Richard L. and Anna J., eds. *Living with the Wall—West Berlin, 1961-1985.* Duke University Press, 1985.

Morton, Edwina, ed. *Germany between East & West.* Cambridge, GB: Cambridge University Press, 1987.

Turner, Henry Ashby. *The Two Germanies since 1945.* Binghamton, NY: Vail-Ballou Press, 1987.

Van Beyme, Klaus, and Manfred G. Schmidt, eds. *Policy and Politics in the Federal Republic of Germany.* New York: St. Martin's Press, 1987.

## IMPORTANT GOVERNMENT PUBLICATIONS

There are three main sources for government publications, principally in the areas of business, economics, and statistics.

### The Department of Commerce

The Department of Commerce publishes a number of reports full of valuable information. Among the highlights:

*Marketing in the Federal Republic of West Germany and West Berlin*

*Foreign Economic Trends and Their Implications for the U.S.: Federal Republic of Germany* (updated every six months)

*Sources of Country Market Information for the Federal Republic of Germany*
Semiannual publication available by subscription from Superintendent of Documents, Government Printing Office, Washington, DC 20402. Single copies may be obtained for a small fee from Publications Sales Branch, Room 1617, U.S. Department of Commerce, Washington, DC 20230. For a complete bibliography of Department of Commerce publications, contact the Country Specialist for the Federal Republic of Germany, Department of Commerce, 14th and Constitution Avenue NW, Washington, DC 20230. Tel: (202) 377-2434.

The U.S. Department of Commerce also publishes reports and information on the European Community. Two offices to contact for listings of materials are

Single Internal Market Information Service, U.S. Department of Commerce, 14th and Constitution Avenue NW, Room 3036, Washington, DC 20230

Office of European Community Affairs, International Trade
Administration, 14th and Constitution Avenue NW, Room H
3036, Washington, DC 20230

The State Department's Public Affairs Office regularly publishes
a concise but very instructive brochure entitled "Background Notes,"
available at most libraries.

## The European Community

The European Community publishes many reports, surveys, and
other studies. To obtain a full listing of materials, contact the Delegation
of the Economic Community, Press and Information, 2100 M Street
NW, Suite 707, Washington, DC 20037. Tel: (202) 862-9500, or
the Commission of the European Communities, 200 rue de la Loi,
B-1049 Brussels, or the Office for Official Publications of the European
Communities, Batiment Jean Monnet, L-2985 Luxembourg.

## The Organization for Economic Cooperation and Development (OECD)

The OECD is another source of abundant documentation, for example,
"OECD Economic Survey: Federal Republic of West Germany."
Publications are sold through OECD, 2001 L Street NW, Suite 700,
Washington, DC 20036. Tel: (202) 785-6323, or through headquar-
ters in Bonn: OECD Publications and Information Center, D-5300
Bonn, 4 Simrackstrasse.

# Appendix

## EUROPEAN AND AMERICAN SCHOOL SYSTEMS: A COMPARISON

European and American educational systems vary greatly at the high school level. European students carry more courses (as many as twelve at a time) at less depth but for more years than their American counterparts. While the end result is comparable, switching between systems in midstream can present difficulties.

## U.S. Curriculum

Schools abroad which offer an American curriculum are on a par with the best Stateside private schools. Course offerings, graduation requirements, textbooks, schedules, and calendars are similar. The curriculum is based on the entrance requirements of the majority of U.S. universities and colleges. The main difference is that more emphasis is placed on the language, art, and history of the area where the school is located. Travel is often an integral part of the curriculum, exposing the students to ideas and cultures different from their own. Student activities and sports programs parallel those in the United States. The quality of college preparation varies from school to school, just as in the U.S., but the student stands as good a chance—if not a better one—of gaining acceptance to the U.S. college of his/her choice from a quality boarding school in Europe as from a high school in the United States. Many colleges consider the international experience to be an advantage. All schools either offer or make arrangements for their students to take PSAT, SAT, and College Board Examinations.

## Accreditation of U.S. Schools

Accreditation applies only to U.S. curriculum schools. Being accredited certifies that a school has met the prescribed standards of quality established by one of the six regional associations of U.S. schools. While many independent day and boarding high schools in the U.S. and abroad are affiliated with one of these associations, accreditation and the resultant association membership is not mandatory. Lack of accreditation does not necessarily imply lack of quality. A school must apply for accreditation—a process of self-study and evaluation, combined with an evaluation by an outside source. This is both costly and time-consuming.

Accreditation does imply several things:

1.  The school's philosophy and goals are soundly conceived and its program is designed to achieve these stated objectives.

2.  The school is implementing its goals and meeting the standards of the regional association.

3.  The school is engaged in a continuous program for improvement.

The main purpose of the accreditation process is the improvement of the educational program, achieved by evaluating the attainment of the educational results defined by the school.

In addition to the six U.S. associations, there are several regional Councils of Overseas Schools, operating under the auspices of the U.S. State Department's Office of Overseas Schools. Membership is limited to those schools offering preparation for U.S. university entrance.

## International Baccalaureate Schools

Many schools, including some in the United States, are now offering an International Baccalaureate Diploma (I.B.) in addition to or instead of U.S., U.K., or other national exams or diplomas. The I.B., established in 1971, is the first program meeting international university entrance requirements. The standards of the I.B. program are higher than those necessary for entrance to most U.S. universities; thus, students having completed the program generally qualify for advanced placement (A.P.) credit on entering a university. The two-year I.B. program offers a demanding curriculum in the major academic fields. High standards are maintained by means of externally administered, thorough examinations.

The I.B. program can provide a challenge for the gifted child, enrich the educational program of the schools, and facilitate the placement of students in universities in the United States and abroad. It is based on the concept of developing "all the powers of the mind through which people interpret, modify and enjoy their environment." For some students, the completion of an I.B. program may require an additional (thirteenth) year of school.

During the two-year program, the I.B. diploma candidate must complete the course work and receive acceptable grades on examinations in six subjects, three at higher level and three at subsidiary level. Higher-level subjects require at least five periods of instruction per week for two years while subsidiary-level subjects require five hours per week for one year or three hours per week for two years. Courses taken at higher level are equivalent to advanced placement. The required courses for completion of the I.B. diploma program are the following:

1. Language A (generally the students' native language)

2. Language B (a second language)

3. Study of humanity (one of the following): history, geography, economics, philosophy, psychology, social anthropology

4. Experimental sciences (one of the following): biology, chemistry, physics, physical science

5. Mathematics

6. One of the following: art, music, a third language, a second subject under number 3 or 4, or further mathematics

The International Baccalaureate program is a structured program offering a strong general education as well as being flexible and acknowledging the individuality of the student.